Copyright

Be sure to check out Mike Riley's other books:

Lost and Missing: True Stories of People Gone Missing and Never Found
"Police launched a massive search, reaching miles away from where the children were last seen in all directions. However, no evidence or any of their belongings were ever found. Even if three children could have been swept out to sea unnoticed on a crowded beach, what happened to their towels, clothes, and other items?"
Check it out on Amazon in the Kindle eBooks Category

Lost and Missing Vol. 2: More True Stories of People Gone Missing and Never Found
"Interestingly, it was discovered that the same day of the three women's disappearance, a concrete foundation was being poured at a hospital nearby. It would have perhaps been an ideal place to dispose of three bodies, but there is no evidence to support any such claim. It's rumored that ground-penetrating radar discovered three anomalies in the set concrete, but it has never been dug up."
Check it out on Amazon in the Kindle eBooks Category

Table of Contents

Introduction

Taking the life of another person is considered by many to be the most evil action taken by human beings. Especially when the victim is an innocent individual, the crime becomes even more heinous. If the perpetrator never comes to justice, our outrage is complete. We wonder about the victim's friends and families. How do they ever get past the horrible event and go on with their lives? How do they ever become whole again. Perhaps they never do.

On the other hand, human tragedies fascinate many people. Whether the cause is environmental, the results of war, of unknown origin or simple accidents, the struggles and sometime triumphs of others make interesting reading.

Following are some stories of people who were murdered and despite the efforts of law enforcement, the culprits have never been brought to justice. I hope you enjoy this volume of fascinating and still unsolved murders.

Al Swearengen: Vicious Deadwood Bar Owner

Victim: Al Swearengen
Date: 1904
Location: Denver, Colorado
Suspect: None

Backstory:
Ellis Alfred Swearengen, nicknamed Al, was born on July 8th, 1845. One of identical twins, and the eldest of eight siblings, he grew up along with his family in Iowa. When he was thirty years old, he settled with his then wife Nettie in Deadwood, arriving in May of 1876. Now a thriving city in South Dakota, Deadwood was originally an illegal settlement on land that had been granted to Native Americans.

Swearengen settled quickly in Deadwood, and within a week he had opened a dance hall. However, his marriage was not to last and by September of the same year Nettie left him. She would later claim that Swearengen had abused her. She continued with abuse claims made against two subsequent husbands, all from Deadwood. However, given what we know of Swearengen's history, it seems likely to be true in his case at least.

Swearengen was not one to sit idle, and he soon replaced the dance hall with a tavern in a permanent building. He also hosted prizefights in the small building, though no official prize was ever actually given.

By 1877 he had set up a theatre in the town. It offered both shows and continued the fights, but it also had a darker side. The theatre also ran as a brothel, and it quickly earned a reputation for how the women were forced into service there and then how they were treated. Advertising for women to perform in the theatre, a very different job would greet them when they arrived. There were also rumors of abuse towards the women, and they were often seen with injuries and bruises.

Supported by many prominent figures in the town, the theatre was left alone to carry on mostly unhindered by law enforcement, despite what went on inside. Looking only at the profits, the theatre was a huge success, bringing in up to the modern equivalent of $280,000 a night. However during a fire in 1879 it burned down, along with most of the town. Swearengen would not be put off and rebuilt an even more opulent building. However, it too burned down in 1899, and this time renewed efforts to clean up the town were having an effect, and so it was not rebuilt.

On The Day In Question:
Only after the theatre was finally closed for good did people begin to speak out against it. In 1899, after the final closure, the local newspaper wrote an article calling it a 'vicious institution' and the 'ever-lasting shame of Deadwood'. However, that seemed to be the end of the matter. Until, on November 15th, 1904, Swearengen was found dead in Denver, Colorado. He was discovered lying near a streetcar track.

Investigation:
Over the years it has often been reported that Swearengen died hopping trains, but an obituary not re-discovered until 2007 instead lists the cause of death as a massive head wound. It was never able to be determined whether the wound was inflicted intentionally or if Swearengen died from an accident. No other evidence or suspects have ever come to light. Did Swearengen simply trip when he alighted from a streetcar, or did his nefarious past in the Deadwood theatre catch up with him? He married three times while in Deadwood, and all three marriages ended in claims of abuse.

After leaving Deadwood at the end of the theatre's reign in 1899, Swearengen went to stay with his twin brother in

Oskaloosa, Iowa. While Al was visiting, his twin was brutally attacked. Lemuel Swearengen had left the market with over $200 on his person when he was shot five times. Perhaps tellingly, despite the large amount of cash he was carrying, he was not robbed. Was this a case of mistaken identity, his attacker really after his identical twin? Lemuel Swearengen survived the attack, but less than two months later Al Swearengen was killed in Colorado.

Interestingly, approximately seven months after Al Swearengen's death, Lemuel was found unconscious, also beaten over the head. He never regained consciousness and died eight days later. Perhaps the killer wanted to make absolutely sure he got the right twin this time.

Current Status:
Al Swearengen's cause of death remains a mystery to this day.

The life and death of Al Swearengen might have disappeared into history, were it not for a new television show on HBO in 2004. Named *Deadwood*, after the town it centers on, it explores the birth of the town and the power struggles that were fought in the early days of the frontier settlement. Al Swearengen is a main character on the show, and despite the immorality the character displays, producers have been quoted as saying the show is too kind to the real Swearengen, who was much, much worse.

The Moore Family: The Villisca Axe Murder Victims

Victims: Josiah and Sarah Moore, their children, Herman, Katherine, Boyd and Paul
and Lena and Ina Stillinger
Date: June 10th, 1912
Location: Villisca, Iowa
Suspects: Frank Jones, Reverend George Kelly

Backstory:
In 1912 Villisca, Iowa was a small town sitting alongside the railway. With a population of less than 1,500 today, in the early 1900's the town was flourishing and busy.

Josiah B. Moore, aged 43 and called J.B., lived there with his wife Sarah, aged 39, and their four children; Herman Montgomery, aged 11, Mary Katherine, aged 9, Arthur Boyd, aged 7, and Paul Vernon, aged 5. J.B. was a successful businessman and well liked in town, selling farm implements to the local residents.

On The Day In Question:
A neighbor was the first to notice a problem. Very early in the morning of June 10th, Mary Peckham was hanging out her washing, trying to avoid the worst of what would be a very hot day. She noticed the home of her neighbors, the Moore family, was shrouded in silence. The family included four children, and the household was usually up and busy early. The livestock were also unattended, and the curtains were still drawn.

Peckham was puzzled, she'd just seen the whole family the night before, and they all seemed well. She tried their door, and found it locked from the inside, something very unusual in the small community. When no one answered her knocking, she went back to her chores, though she was still concerned. Eventually, her worries must have increased, and she contacted her neighbor's brother, Ross Moore.

Moore first called J.B. Moore's workplace, but the manager at the pharmacy hadn't seen him. So, now worried himself, he went to the house to check on the family. He found the livestock fed and relaxed. What he didn't know at the time however was that Peckham, noticing that the animals were still unattended to, had asked a friend to do it.

However, Moore decided that he needed to enter the house. Thankfully, he had his own key and was able to let himself in, with Peckham following. He walked through the first two rooms on the ground floor, but found nothing. Steeling his nerves, he opened the bedroom door, and then came rushing out calling for Peckham to fetch the sheriff.

Back then, only large towns had official police forces, and so the man who came to the scene was John Henry "Hank" Horton, who was the town's appointed peace officer. In 1912, most law enforcement had very little training, and evidence was a very different ballgame. Fingerprints were only just becoming known to the legal system, and peace officers had little to no training on how to handle a crime scene or preserve evidence.

Horton entered the bedroom and immediately saw blood spatters on the walls. The bed still contained two people, lying very still, with only one arm from one of the victims extended from the bed. No doubt due in part to the heat of the day, you could already smell the death in the room.

Upon lighting the room with a small glow from a match, he found an axe leaning up against the wall. It too was covered in dark stains. Horton then exited the bedroom and proceeded up the staircase. By then however, another brother of J.B.'s, along with another man had already entered the house, and the scene was compromised.

Lighting another match to find his way up the stairs, Horton could again smell blood and death in the air. Upon entering the bedroom upstairs, he found the bodies of J.B. and Sarah Moore. He opened a curtain to let in more light, and found that they had both been the victims of heavy blows to the head, apparently while they were sleeping. Noting a lamp left on the floor, he at least knew enough to not touch it, and he continued his search.

Entering a second upstairs bedroom, he made perhaps the most gruesome discovery of all. In the room were three small beds, and in the beds he found four children, all dead. Blood soaked the beds and covered the room, even spattered onto the ceiling.

Not one family-member survived the attack. However, a terrible thought struck Horton. The family that lived in the house was J.B. and Sarah Moore, and their four children. Who were the two bodies downstairs?

Investigation:
Horton was quickly realizing that the case would be a headliner. He planned on calling the town's physician to help him officially confirm the identities of the bodies in the downstairs bedroom. Although axes were not uncommon as a weapon at that time, the single killing of an entire family at once was nearly unheard of. How had the killer managed to overwhelm the entire family at once? Perhaps there was more than one killer. Horton knew that he was out of his depth with this case.

By now it was nearly 9:00AM, and in the small town the news had spread like wildfire. The Moores were a well off and much liked family in the town, and the news of the killings was quickly spreading.

One family who heard the news was the Stillingers, who had let their two daughters Lena (12) and Ina (8) sleep over at the house. As they were just becoming concerned as to the whereabouts of their children, they heard from a telephone operator that everyone at the house was dead. How could they even believe it?

The physician, Dr. Cooper, soon arrived and entered the house. He was not alone however. As well as Horton, two other doctors and a Reverend all entered the house, further degrading the scene. Soon after, the county coroner Dr. A. L. Linquist also entered the house to oversee the identifications.

In the downstairs bedroom, the faces of the victims were so damaged from the attack that no one could recognize them. Oddly, a gray boys coat had been placed over the face of one of the children. The elder of the children appeared to have been sexually abused before death, or at the very least posed after death. They were identified as Ina and Lena Stillinger based on personal belongings lying near the bead. Were they the target of the attack, or simply in the wrong place at the wrong time?

Continuing upstairs, it was determined that every member of the Moore family had been killed in the same way as the girls downstairs. First they had been struck with the dull side of the axe, likely stunning them, and the killer had then used the sharp edge to deliver the fatal blow. Only one axe was found at the scene, the one in the downstairs bedroom, and so it was assumed that the single weapon was used for each killing.

J.B. Moore had suffered the most, struck over the head repeatedly in a massive overkill. Was he the primary target, or simply as the only adult male in the house, was more required to subdue him? In comparison, the Moore children were treated almost reverently, in some cases with clothes or gauze placed over the wounds.

A few strange pieces of evidence were found in the bedroom on the ground floor. The coroner found four pounds of bacon and a keychain on the floor of the room. There was a second similar sized piece of bacon still in the icebox, which had been broken. On the table were a bowl of bloody water and a full plate of food, which had been prepared but not eaten.

Several mirrors in the house had been covered with clothing or clothes, and a single shoe belonging to Sarah Moore was found on the floor near J.B. Moore's side of the bed. The shoe was likely moved by the killer and was filled with blood. The coroner decided that blood from Moore's considerable head injury had dripped down into the shoe, steadily filling it.

Finally, the axe had been partially wiped clean with cloth found on the scene. The killer had also attempted to clean his hands, the investigators finding bloody handprints on several items. On searching the rest of the property, Linquist reported finding a sort of depression in a bundle of hay in the barn. He believed it to be recent and indicated that someone had been lying there recently. Positioned there, whoever it was would have had a full view of the house.

As well as so many law enforcement and related persons in the house, curious townsfolk had by now also arrived, and despite orders to keep away, many of them had entered the house. Finally by 12:00PM the National Guard arrived and started to control the scene. By then however it was already irreparably damaged. The bodies were finally removed from the house just before midnight, and they were released for burial.

By that evening, a bloodhound arrived from Nebraska, in hopes of tracking any trail left behind by the killer. However by then so many people unrelated to the case had been through the house, and had handled the axe, that getting a scent was a nearly impossible task. The dogs sniffed with interest along one side of a river, but lost the scent after that and found no scent on the other side of the river. If it was even the killer's scent they were following, he was long gone.

After federal assistance was requested, one of the country's few fingerprint analysis experts arrived. M.W. McClaughry, who was the Special Agent in Charge of the Department of Justice, processed the whole house. Again however, with so many people touching the axe and other things inside the house, not a single clear print could be found.

Sadly, in the week following the murders, Mrs. Stillinger, who had been pregnant at the time her other children were killed, gave birth to a stillborn baby. Perhaps the stress had simply been too much.

As the murders were investigated, many suspects were interviewed, but none were charged with any offense. A lack of physical evidence, including confusion regarding clues such as the meal left out and the bacon, meant that it was difficult to pin down any clear motive or suspect.

With science as it was at the time, investigators could not even tell who had been attacked first. Criminologists today believe that there was likely a sexual aspect to the crimes, and the bacon was used as a bizarre masturbation aid, but in 1912 this was not even considered.

They did know that the crime had taken place sometime between midnight and 5:00AM. The axe was identified as belonging to the family. Had it simply been a crime of opportunity? Lamps in the house had been dimmed to just barely flickering. Whatever the motive, the killer had made sure that no light would be seen from outside the home while he was inside.

Although the weapon was silent, the swings had embedded the axe in the walls, and at some points also the stairs and ceilings. How was it none of the victims heard anything before they too were attacked?

Why had most of the victims had their faces covered, as well as the mirrors in the home? It was a common belief at the time that the last thing you saw could be imprinted on your retina upon death, and so perhaps the killer was trying to protect his identity. In some cultures, mirrors are turned around or covered after death, so that the wandering soul does not become trapped.

Another possibility however is that he knew his victims and felt regret, particularly upon killing the children. The overkill used also signified a personal relationship with the victims. Usually such vicious killings indicated a personal grudge or anger towards the victim.

Due to this theory, suspicion first fell on Moore's ex business partner. At first Frank Jones had worked with Moore, but they had split and Moore had taken some of Jones's largest customers. Now a politician, Jones had the means and contacts necessary to organize the killings.

Adding fuel to the fire was the rumor that Jones's daughter had been involved in an affair with J.B. Moore. One of the investigators even accused Jones outright, but he denied having anything to do with the whole situation.

Given the bizarre clues around the scene and the frenzied attack, investigators also wondered whether the killer had some kind of mental illness. Perhaps Mrs. Moore had attracted a stalker, who had been watching her from the spot in the hay in the barn.

By the next day, investigators had all but concluded that the murders were not the work of anyone local and had been committed by a roving homicidal maniac. They considered the possibility of a link to other axe murders that occurred nine months previously in Colorado Springs, around seven hundred miles from Villisca. There too, whole families had been slaughtered in their sleep. The attacks continued in various places, like Illinois and Kansas, and one just one week before the Moore family murders.

Unfortunately at that time the concept of a serial killer was still in its infancy, and while the cases had some similarities, investigators also believed they had key differences. While it was recognized that a single person could engage in repeated murders, particularly across different jurisdictions, proving it with the technology and resources at the time remained very difficult.

In fact, many suspects did eventually come to light, including information from a psychic in a nearby village (that later did not pan out) and a mentally ill preacher who ended up becoming obsessed with the murders. He allegedly confessed some years later.

Six months after the Villisca murders, a man named Henry Moore (unrelated to the murdered family) was arrested after killing his wife and grandmother with an axe in Missouri. M.W. McClaughry investigated the possibility he was also connected to the Villisca killings, along with other unsolved axe murders.

After interviewing Moore in prison, McClaughry later declared that he was the killer in an astounding twenty-three different murders. However, and perhaps even more astonishingly, no one else every followed up and Moore was never charged or prosecuted for a single one.

So what of a hit man theory? A man by the name of William Mansfield, who had been associated with Moore's ex business partner Jones, became a suspect in another axe murder two years after the Moore's deaths. It was in fact the death of Mansfield's own family – his wife, child and in-laws. He was also suspected in some of the killings that McClaughry had accused Henry Moore of committing.

Although there were only rumors, by the year 1916, suspicion was so strong that Mansfield was arrested and the case was brought before a grand jury. However, before any charges could be laid, he produced payroll records proving he had been in Illinois when the Moore family was murdered. Mansfield was released without charge.

Another suspect was a man by the name of Andy Sawyer. He had been seen on June 10th caked in mud, perhaps wading through the river to escape bloodhounds? He also was very vocal in his interest in the case and allegedly feared that he would become a suspect himself. He apparently took an axe to bed for his own protection, and was quite skilled at wielding it. As with Mansfield however, he was able to prove he'd been in another town when the crimes were committed, and he was never formally investigated or charged.

So what of the Reverend who was obsessed with the case? He was a small man, standing at only just over five feet tall. Was it even possible he could have committed the crimes, given his lack of physical strength? Reverend Lyn George J. Kelly had arrived in the town only a few days before, on the 8th of June, and left the day after the horrific crime was discovered.

It may seem suspicious, but he was a travelling preacher and could have been already scheduled to leave that day. However, it was clear from his behavior while in town that he'd been uncomfortable running the children's program at the church, in which all the murdered children had participated.

Also raising suspicions against him is a witness stating that Kelly had allegedly told some people on his early morning train that there had been people killed that morning in

Villisca. The problem is that he was alleged to have spoken about the crimes at 7:00AM, before any of the bodies had been discovered. Gossip about Kelly said that he had received a vision to kill the family.

He also had a reputation as a peeping tom. Investigations of the crime scene lead investigators to believe that the killer was left-handed, of which only around 10% of the world's population is, including Reverend Kelly. That observation, when discovered at his confession in 1917, was just about the proverbial nail in the coffin for the Reverend.

Revered Kelly was taken to trial, but before it could begin he recanted his confession. His attorney, W.E. Mitchell, also challenged it in court by claiming that it only occurred after a full night of intensive interrogation. He also claimed it was being used by investigators to protect the true killer. Mitchell suggested that political connections were giving the real perpetrator a shield.

Kelly's trial began in September of 1917, with the main defense strategy being to use the business partner Jones as reasonable doubt. During the trial, it came to light that in 1914 Kelly had been questioned and arrested in South Dakota for sending obscene materials through the post. During that interview, Kelly had made a similar confession. A jailhouse snitch that Kelly shared a cell with testified that Kelly had confessed to him as well.

Therefore, Mitchell's tactic switched to proving that Kelly was so obsessed with the killings that he imagined himself as the attacker. Allegedly in 1912 he'd been so interested in the murders that he claimed he'd received training as a detective from Scotland Yard. His wife also gave evidence, testifying that her husband had a history of false confessions, and was of 'weak mind'.

With the only other evidence to consider being Kelly's left-handedness and his apparent dislike of children, the verdict resulted in a hung jury, with one juror wanting to find him not guilty for reason of insanity. The other eleven men wanted to acquit him outright.

He went to trial for a second time and this time was acquitted. The prosecutors had tried him only for the murder of Lena Stillinger, perhaps hoping that they could skate the edges of double jeopardy and keep trying him for each murder until one stuck.

However, no further trials ever happened, and as far as can be ascertained Reverend Kelly eventually lived out his days in a psychiatric hospital. Did he get away with murder, or did the Villisca killer hop a train and continue to cross America, killing along the way?

Current Status:
Modern profiling by former FBI profiler Robert Ressler has created a possible description of the killer. He suggested that the killer would have been a larger and more powerful man, most likely in his mid to late thirties. He would have had some kind of mental illness, but would not have stood out as having a full-blown psychosis.

After Henry Moore was in prison for the unrelated axe murder of his family, the series of axe murders that had occurred across the east coast of America ceased. While not definitive proof of guilt, this, along with Ressler's profile, certainly suggests that he may have been the perpetrator   all   along.

Surprisingly, the Moore house still stands today. Since the murders, it's been owned by at least eight different parties. The house slowly deteriorated over the years until in 1994, it was renovated by new owners Darwin and Martha Linn. The Linn's purposely staged it reflect how it would have appeared on the day of the murders.

With the original furniture long gone, they dressed the house with antiques similar to what would have been found in the original house. The house is now on the National Register of Historic Places and is open for tours. Many ghost hunters have attended, and reports of oil lamps self-extinguishing, hearing falling objects and children's voices persist to this day.

Julia Wallace: A Husband's Plot?

Victim: Julia Wallace
Date: January 20th, 1931
Location: Liverpool, England
Suspect: William Wallace

Backstory:
Julia Wallace (nee Dennis) was born on April 28th, 1861. She met her husband, William Herbert Wallace when he was working for the UK's Liberal Party in Harrogate, England. She married Wallace in March of 1914. Originally, it was believed that the couple was the same age. However, in 2001 her original birth certificate was uncovered, and we now know that she was seventeen years older than her husband.

When the First World War began, William Wallace's position as the Liberal election agent was discontinued. Elections were suspended and a parliamentary truce had been called, and so he was out of a job. Wallace was able to find new work as a collections agent with a life insurance company, and in 1915 the couple moved to Liverpool. Wallace supplemented the family income by lecturing part time at a local technical college. He also learned violin to accompany Julia, who was an accomplished pianist and hosted musical evenings at their home.

On The Day In Question:
The unusual circumstances surrounding this case actually began the day before the main event. On January 19th, 1931 someone placed an evening phone call to a chess club in Liverpool, asking for William Wallace. Wallace was a member, but as yet had not arrived at the club, and so a message was taken. The caller asked to tell him that a man named R. M. Qualtrough requested Mr. Wallace to visit him at home the next day to discuss an insurance policy. The address given was Menlove Gardens East. The rest of the evening passed without incident.

The next evening, William Wallace left home to go to his appointment. Julia Wallace remained at home. He knew of the street Menlove Gardens West, and so assumed that the East version must be nearby. When he arrived however, he could find no street with that name. After wandering around for some time, he asked both shopkeepers and police, and was informed by all of them that the address did not exist. Becoming confused by this point, he had another brief look around and then cut his losses and headed back home.

When he arrived, he reportedly tried to enter using his key and failed. The front door was dead bolted from the inside. He tried the backdoor, but found it locked in the same way. The house was dark, with no lights on inside. He tried both doors again, and on his second attempt was able to unlock the back door. Had someone unbolted it, or did he make a mistake the first time around?

Entering the house, Mr. Wallace turned on lights as he progressed through the rooms. As he made his way into the sitting room, a grisly find awaited him. There on the floor lay Julia Wallace. She had been hit repeatedly with a blunt weapon and was already dead. Wallace immediately called out to a neighbor, who then called the police.

When they arrived, the police found very little evidence. A small amount of money was missing, but not enough to conclusively label robbery as the motive. The only other clues were some missing fireplace implements; both a poker and metal bar were gone and presumed to be the murder weapons.

Investigation:
As with many murders, police investigated William Wallace, the victim's husband. He made two voluntary statements to the police, however in the first two weeks after the fateful night, he was never fully interrogated. He

was however required to visit the police headquarters daily. The police questioned him about whether they employed household staff, questions about the identity of the mystery caller at the chess club, and whether perhaps he had met or spoken to anyone specific while looking for the address.

Whether or not they made it clear to Wallace at the time, police were beginning to suspect that the man named Qualtrough had been Wallace himself all along, giving himself an alibi for why he was away from the house that night. Despite shopkeepers around the area confirming he had really been walking the streets around the time of the attack, two weeks after that night, William Wallace was arrested for the murder of his wife.

Police tried to prove that it was possible for Wallace to have committed the crime and still made the trip to the non-existent street. They tested this by having a young, fit detective go through the same motions as the murder, and then sprint down to the tram stop. This would likely have been impossible for Wallace, who was aged fifty-two and also of ill health. Perhaps in an effort to make the crime fit the suspect, the time of death was also revised down from 8:00PM to 6:30PM, though no new evidence was provided to explain the change.

Forensic evidence suggests that there was no way that Julia Wallace's attacker could have been anything but covered in blood after the murder. Police closely examined the clothing Wallace was wearing that night, but found nothing unusual. Interestingly, a raincoat was found under Julia Wallace's body at the crime scene.

Police suggested that Wallace had stripped naked and then dressed in the raincoat, explaining the lack of blood on his clothing. However, there was no blood found in any of the drains in the house. Surely he would still have had to wash his face and hands after such a brutal attack? A further search found a single blood clot in the toilet pan, but why it was there was never definitively established.

Despite only circumstantial evidence and constant denials by William Wallace, he was charged with his wife's murder. During trial, despite a potential alibi witness stating Wallace had spoken to Julia only moments before he would have had to be on the tram, the jury found Wallace guilty after only one hour's deliberation. Not only that, he was sentenced to death.

Almost as amazing as the verdict itself, the Court of Criminal Appeal then quashed it, reporting that it was not supported by the weight of the evidence. Usually, appeals were brought based on allegation of bad decisions by judges or new evidence emerging. This time, the appeal court's actions meant that they believed the jury was wrong, and it was also the first time a conviction of murder had been overturned. William Wallace walked away a free man.

Current Status:
Despite being found not guilty, or rather having his conviction quashed, his life as William Wallace knew it was over. He returned to his job, but many in the local area still considered him guilty and he was shunned by both existing and potential customers. After receiving hate mail and physical threats, he took a desk job with his employer. He was still employed by the same company when he died in 1933.

There have been other suspects over time. Famous authors, including John Gannon and PD James, both profess to have investigated and solved the case. James believes that a local twenty-two year old man named Richard Parry placed the prank call with the false address to Wallace. Wallace worked with Parry, and had informed on him when Wallace discovered he'd fiddled with the books at their employer, and Parry was fired. James believes that Parry intended to send him on a wild goose chase as revenge. James does however believe that ultimately Wallace was still responsible for the actual murder.

Gannon hypothesizes that Wallace, knowing that he was ill and did not have long to live, wanted out of his marriage ASAP. He suggests that Wallace was in cahoots with Parry, persuading him to make the prank call, rather than it being a revenge plot that Wallace had no knowledge of. This provided Wallace with an alibi, and he then convinced a third man named Joseph Caleb Marsden to actually kill his wife.

Marsden was very well connected in society, and in fact was about to marry even better. According to Gannon, Julia had been paying Marsden for sex, and William Wallace knew it. He theorizes that Marsden was blackmailed into the murder to protect his upcoming marriage chances being destroyed.

Wallace himself did drop both Marsden and Parry's names to the police at the time of the investigation. Despite this, neither was ever named as suspects. Wallace suggested to investigators that Parry would know his takings for the day would be at his home, giving him motive. However, when they investigated, police were satisfied with Parry's alibi. In addition, it appears that although Wallace name-dropped Marsden as someone his wife would have let into the house when she was alone, the police never gave him a close look.

Because of Wallace's quashed conviction, officially, the case remains unsolved. The court of popular opinion for William Wallace however may tell a different story.

Lilly Lindestrom: A Vampire Murder

Victim: Lilly Lindestrom
Date: May 4th, 1932
Location: Stockholm, Sweden
Suspect: None

Backstory:
Although the case of the murder of Lilly Lindestrom is possibly one of the strangest unsolved murder mysteries, we know very little about what actually happened that fateful night.

Lindestrom was thirty-two years old, and lived in Stockholm, Sweden. She was a divorcee and worked as a prostitute, but nothing more is really known about her, other than the strange way in which she died.

On The Day In Question:
On May 4th, 1932, Lindestrom was found dead in her apartment. She had already been dead for several days when her body was discovered. Her body had been left lying face down on her bed.

Reports indicated she had died from blunt force trauma to the head. We know she had been involved in sexual activity shortly before her death, as a condom was found still protruding from her anus. It's not known whether it was consensual or not, or who her visitor was.

With the investigation of the larger crime scene, the case was about to get very strange. Investigators found a gravy ladle at the scene – not something that you'd usually expect to find at a murder scene.

Then, as Lindestrom's body was further examined, they noticed that she had been drained of at least some, and possibly all, of her blood. Had the killer used the ladle to sip at his macabre drink?

Investigation:
Further investigation revealed that the last person to see Lindestrom alive was a friend named Minnie Jasson. It's believed that Jasson lived in the flat near or below Lindestrom, but this is not absolutely clear.

Jasson told investigators that one evening, Lindestrom had visited her twice to ask for condoms. The second time she visited, Lindestrom was completely naked under her overcoat. She had not seen any sign of Lindestrom since that night.

After receiving no response when she rang the doorbell, Jasson had rung the police, and they had entered to find Lindestrom's dead body. Along with the strangeness of the ladle, police found Lindestrom's clothes folded neatly on a chair near her body. Had she been entertaining a paying guest, only to have him turn the tables on her expectations of the evening?

Police investigated eighty of Lindestrom's past customers, but no suspect was ever made public, nor was any forensic evidence found at the scene.

Current Status:
Due to the strange nature of her death, Lindestrom's murder is still discussed today. The lack of any fingerprints at the scene have led some to believe that the killer was someone with crime scene experience, a policeman perhaps, who knew to wipe evidence down and cover his tracks.

Whoever was truly responsible, whether her last customer was the killer or was simply with Lindestrom just before her final moments, they can likely shed light on the case. However, he has never been found.

Georgette Bauerdorf: The Hostess and the Soldier

Victim: Georgette Bauerdorf
Date: October 11th, 1944
Location: Hollywood, California
Suspect: An unknown American soldier

Backstory:
Georgette Elise Bauerdorf was born on May 6th, 1924. She was a socialite from a rich oil family. The younger of two daughters, Bauerdorf was born in New York City. She attended the private girls school St. Agatha's. However, after her mother died when she was eleven years old, the family moved to Los Angeles.

As she grew up, Bauerdorf decided she wanted to become an actress, and in 1944 when she was twenty years old, she moved to Hollywood. She found an apartment and a job working as a hostess at the Hollywood Canteen, a popular club that offered food and entertainment for U.S. servicemen.

The club was owned by Bette Davis, John Garfield, and Jules Stein. Stars volunteered at the club, and one of the highlights for the servicemen (often heading out to active duty) was to dance with a celebrity. Bauerdorf was also a dancer at the club.

On The Day In Question:
On October 10th, 1944, Bauerdorf cashed a check for $175 and used the money to purchase a plane ticket going to El Paso, Texas. Friends were told that she was going to visit her boyfriend, who was a soldier. The mystery man was later identified as Pvt. Jerome M. Brown, who was an anti-aircraft artillery trainee and had met Bauerdorf at the club.

The next day, on October 11th, we believe that Bauerdorf left the Hollywood Canteen around 11:15PM, and went straight home. Previous to working that evening, she'd had lunch with her father's secretary, a woman named Rose L. Gilbert. Gilbert reported to police that after lunch, the pair had gone shopping. Bauerdorf was in a good mood, and nothing indicated she had any inkling of what was to come.

It's not known if anyone saw Bauerdorf after she left work. What is known is that on October 12th, a maid arrived to clean Bauerdorf's apartment, and found more than she bargained for. Bauerdorf's dead body was lying face down in an overflowing bath.

Investigation:
Early examination of the crime scene found that a sensor light outside Bauerdorf's front door had been unscrewed just enough to make it fail to turn on, but not enough that you would notice anything amiss.

Fingerprints were found on the bulb, and whoever unscrewed it would have had to stand on a chair at least to reach it. It seemed that the attack was planned and deliberate.

Further evidence supported the theory of someone laying in wait. Investigators found an empty can of string beans in the kitchen bin, along with some melon rinds. Later examination of her stomach contents would indicate that it was Bauerdorf who had eaten the beans. Had the attacker been waiting in her room while she sat in the kitchen indulging in a midnight snack?

Robbery did not appear to be a motive. No valuables or jewelry were stolen. Approximately $100 was taken from her purse, but perhaps this was meant as a distraction, as there was a large amount of money and other valuables left lying in plain sight.

What was missing was a car, registered in Bauerdorf's sister's name, Connie. The car was later located, but with fresh damage to a fender. The car had apparently run out of gas and been abandoned when it stopped running.

An examination of Bauerdorf's body showed that she hadn't gone quietly. The surgeon performing the autopsy found many bruises and scratches over her body. Her right hand was also bruised and her knuckles were broken. She also had bruises on her head and abdomen, perhaps as the result of punches.

The clear outline of a hand was bruised into her thigh, indicating that at one point she had been forcefully held down. Finally, she had been strangled with a towel, the surgeon finding a piece of it inside her throat. Strangely, the apartment itself did not reflect her fight, showing no signs of a struggle.

Investigators believed that either someone had been lying in wait, or had set the scene with the malfunctioning light and returned after Bauerdorf was in bed. Either way, the case was strong for premeditated murder.

A neighbor reported hearing screams around 2:30AM, but assumed it to be a domestic argument and went back to bed. The general beliefs over intervening in domestic abuse in the 1940's were very different than today.

Investigations first turned towards servicemen that Bauerdorf knew through her work at the club. A date book was found inside her house with several names listed. The Sheriff's Department joined forces with the Army to interview those named, but no suspects were identified. They also scrutinized her mail and also questioned anyone who may have seen someone leaving the club with her.

One particular man came to light. He cut in on nearly every dance Bauerdorf had with someone else on the same night as her death. Initial searches did not find him, but the solider shortly thereafter turned himself in for questioning and police reported that he was exonerated of any crime. However, the mystery man was never named.

A good friend of Bauerdorf's, June Ziegler, told the investigators that Bauerdorf had dated a serviceman a month before her murder. She described him as being tall at 6 foot 4 inches, and friends with another serviceman whose name had been listed in Bauerdorf's date book.

Ziegler reported that the tall solider was much more interested in a relationship than Bauerdorf had been, and she had broken it off. The army searched for the man for questioning.

Ziegler also told investigators that Bauerdorf never entertained men alone for very long. Although she may have invited them in briefly, her strict upbringing gave her a strong sense of propriety. Had someone felt led on, or perhaps wanted more than Bauerdorf was willing to give?

On the 20th of October a coroner's inquest was held, and a jury found that the cause of Bauerdorf's death was homicide. New evidence also emerged during the hearing. A janitor from Bauerdorf's apartment mentioned that he heard a woman's footsteps followed by a loud crash around midnight. However, he did not think anyone else was in the apartment with Bauerdorf at the time.

Current Status:
Bauerdorf's case, while never solved, has been linked to another homicide, that of actress Elizabeth Short in 1947. While the two cases did not have a great deal in common, there were enough similarities that an author writing about Short's case decades later made the connection.

He discovered that both women went to the Hollywood Canteen, and they knew each other. In fact, they looked so alike that some people even mistook one for the other. After never finding a motive or killer, was it possible that

Bauerdorf's murder was a simple case of mistaken identity?

Short was murdered just one year after Bauerdorf, and both crime scenes showed anger and brutality towards the women. Elizabeth Short had a reputation of being a tease that would not sleep with men, but would freely perform oral sex.

Did they attract the same offender, or was Bauerdorf simply in the wrong place at the wrong time and attracted unwanted attention meant for Short? We will likely never know.

Evelyn Hartley: The Homecoming Babysitter

Victim: Evelyn Hartley
Date: October 24th, 1953
Location: La Crosse, Wisconsin
Suspects: Ed Gein

Backstory:
Evelyn Hartley was a fifteen year-old teenager, living in La Crosse, Wisconsin with her parents Richard and Ethel Hartley. La Crosse was a family town, typical of those portrayed in television shows of the 1950's.

The houses were freshly painted, dad went to work while mom stayed at home, and the whole family went to church on Sundays. The town was very patriotic, and had just celebrated its centenary five years earlier.

They were different times than today, and no one was concerned with children riding their bikes across town, even after dark. No one worried about children Hartley's age walking home after a football game. No one even locked the doors.

Babysitting was a popular way for teen girls to earn extra money, then paid just 25 cents an hour. The local college, La Crosse State University, at which Hartley's father was a biology professor, had only 945 students, and life was like any other small American town.

Her friends and family described Hartley as a mature and responsible young woman. She was a straight-A student, and a member of several clubs at her high school. In October of 1953, she was a junior.

As well as doing well at school, Hartley also both played the piano and sang in the choir at her church. She had dated a couple of boys, but did not have a steady boyfriend.

On The Day In Question:
That October, Homecoming was a particularly big deal. La Crosse State was honoring Ted Levenhagen, who had become a local hero for leading the unbeaten lacrosse team. He had been named as an All-American team member in 1952, the first person from La Crosse to receive national recognition. As the team was so far undefeated, tickets to the big game were one of the hottest of the season.

A physics professor at the university, Viggo Rasmusen was taking his wife and seven year-old daughter to the game and needed a babysitter for their twenty month-old daughter. Their usual babysitter, Janice Cowley, the daughter of another professor, was planning to attend the game herself, and so Rasmusen asked Evelyn Hartley to take the job that night.

Wanting to make the most of her time, Hartley had plans to study while the baby slept, and when Rasmusen picked her up she was carrying five schoolbooks and wearing her glasses.

The Rasmusen family lived in a brand new house built in a safe neighborhood. However, it was so new that in some places large amounts of open space and roads without curbs still existed. Streetlights had not yet been installed and the new home was surrounded by a wooded area. Mrs. Rasmusen put the baby to bed herself before they left at 6:45PM. All that Hartley needed to do was settle into her studying.

Both of Hartley's parents remained at the family home that night. It's reported that around 8:00PM, Ethel Hartley experienced an odd feeling that something was wrong. She didn't have anything specific to go on, but mentioned to her husband that they should give Evelyn a call.

Like many parents of a teenager however, they were trying to tread the line between keeping her safe and being overprotective. This was also exacerbated by the earlier death of their older son from polio while he was in training with the Navy in 1946.

Ethel decided not to call, and it was a decision that she would come to regret for the rest of her life. At the time however, Hartley had been gone for only half an hour, and was due to call and check in her self in a short while at 8:30PM.

This was a standing arrangement with her parents whenever she was babysitting. The Hartley's settled down to listen to the football game's radio broadcast, celebrating the local team's latest win.

It was 9:00PM when Hartley's parents realized that they hadn't heard from her, and they started to worry. Her father tried ringing the Rasmusen's phone, but there was no answer. He looked up the number to make sure he had it correct and tried again, with the same result.

Next, he phoned friends and neighbors of the Rasmusens, but none of them had seen Hartley either. Worry increasing, he thought to himself that perhaps the baby was unsettled and Hartley was attending to her, or she was in the bathroom. He decided to go over to the house and check on his daughter himself.

When Richard Hartley arrived at his colleague's house, it didn't look sinister. The lights were on, front door locked, and music was playing inside. He rang the doorbell at the front door, and when there was no answer, repeated the action at the back, but still nothing. He then started banging at the door and shouting out to Evelyn, but his calls continued to go unanswered.

Walking around the exterior of the house again, he discovered that a basement window was unlocked, the metal framing warped. He also noticed that the window screen had been removed and was leaning up against the house.

It was at that point that Richard Hartley decided he needed to enter the house himself, and climbed in through the already open window.

Surprisingly, a ladder was already placed against the wall inside, allowing him to climb down from the window easily. He would later learn that the ladder was not placed there by the perpetrator, but it no doubt gave him easy access.

Likely already worried, what he saw next must have sent Richard Hartley into a full on panic. At the foot of the basement stairs lay a single one of Hartley's shoes. He ran upstairs, only to find her other shoe and glasses. There was no sign of Evelyn Hartley herself. Her books were scattered across the room, and there were smears of blood on the carpet.

He checked on the baby, and found her safe in her crib, adding to the confusion of the scene. At this point there seemed no other option. Someone had entered the house and taken Evelyn Hartley.

Investigation:
After his grim discoveries inside the house, Richard Hartley immediately ran across the street to ask for help. A neighbor named Frank Lindner called the police, handing the phone to Hartley to speak to them. Quickly, twenty officers arrived at the home, with the County Sheriff, the Undersheriff, highway police, detectives and District Attorneys following soon afterwards.

An investigation of the scene showed that there were marks on three other windows, making it appear that someone had tried multiple times to enter the house. Footprints made from tennis shoes were also found in the window box of the basement, and in the living room.

Along with the splatters on the living room carpet, significant amounts of blood were found elsewhere on the premises. Later identified as belonging to Hartley, blood was found inside the home, at the foot of the basement window, and again outside in the yard.

One of the blood pools in the yard was eighteen inches in diameter, and a bloody handprint was also found on the wall of a garage about one hundred feet from the home.

The print was only around four feet from the ground, and the stains continued onto a neighbor's house. Tracker dogs were able to scent Hartley for two blocks before they lost the trail. It was looking likely that Hartley had been transported from there in a car or other vehicle.

Another neighbor reported seeing a light-colored car that seemed to be circling the neighborhood, driving through around 8:00PM. Screams were also reported as occurring around 7:00PM, but the witness had assumed they belonged to children playing. It took an additional two days for another witness to come forward.

A man named Ed Hofer said that around 7:15PM that evening he'd noticed a green Buick speeding away to the west. In the car he saw two men and a girl. Earlier that evening, he'd seen the same people that had been in the car staggering down the street. He'd assumed they were going to the homecoming game, and hadn't thought any more of it until he'd heard about Hartley's abduction.

Around the same time, a pair of bloodstained, size eleven tennis shoes were found southeast of town, in the Coon Valley area. The sole pattern was similar to that found in the Rasmusen house, and their condition indicated that they had likely only been there for a short time before they were discovered.

The blood type matched Hartley's. Inside one of the shoes investigators found a single human hair, identified as possibly coming from someone of African-American descent. Wear patterns on the shoes led investigators to believe that the owner worked with machinery and also rode a motorbike.

It was also later determined that in fact at some time two different people had worn the shoes, the second person's feet being too big for them to fit properly.

Near the shoes, a size thirty-six denim jacket was found, also covered in bloodstains. The jacket had flecks of metal paint on it, possibly tying it to the wearer of the shoes. However, it seemed too small for someone who wore size eleven shoes.

It had a wear mark running around the entire jacket under the arms, consistent with someone wearing a safety harness repeatedly. Again, the blood was determined to belong to Hartley.

The disappearance of a well-liked, responsible local girl sparked one of the largest police searches in the state's history. Investigators left no stone unturned, undertaking a mass search of all local vehicles.

They even interviewed every student and staff member at Hartley's school, including giving each one a polygraph test. The shoes and jacket were displayed in thirty-one different communities in the surrounding area, but no one ever came forward with any clues.

Current Status:
Over the years, many potential suspects were interviewed, but no one was ever charged and no further evidence was

found. That was until the discovery of the crimes of Edward Theodore Gein, a serial killer who first came to the attention of authorities in 1957.

As well as killing victims, Gein was also a grave robber, and when he was arrested police found furniture and accessories in his house made from human remains. Gein has inspired such fictional characters as Norman Bates and the novel *The Silence of the Lambs*.

Some years later, it was discovered that Gein had been in La Crosse visiting relatives, and staying just blocks from the Rasmusen house when Hartley went missing. He was questioned by police, but denied having anything to do with her disappearance.

Police were also unable to find any physical evidence linking back to Hartley at his house, however many people still believe he must have been involved.

Another possible lead came from an audiotape that was rediscovered in 2003. On the tape, a man had been recorded talking about taking Hartley to La Farge, a town around 40 miles from La Crosse, Wisconsin, and then digging a grave.

The tape was sent to a crime lab in Wisconsin for further analysis. It was also tested for DNA, but nothing was found.

Officially, the case remains open.

The Grimes Sisters: Two Lives Cut Short

Victims: Barbara & Patricia Grimes
Dates: Sometime between December 28, 1956 and January 27, 1957
Location: Brighton Park, Chicago
Suspects: Edward Lee "Bennie" Bedwell, Max Fleig, Walter Kranz, Silas Jayne, Charles Melquist

Backstory:
Barbara and Patricia Grimes were sisters who lived with their mother and four other siblings in Brighton Park, Chicago. The mother, Loretta, worked as a clerk for Parke Davis Co. and their father Joseph was a truck driver.

Their parents had married young, when their father was barely seventeen, and by 1956, their parents had already been divorced for eleven years. Their father had remarried.

Loretta Grimes worked long hours at her job. The family had reportedly been on welfare for some of the children's lives, and the family home would sometimes be without heat or electricity.

Patricia Grimes, the younger of the two sisters, was an enthusiastic girl, described as having an impish smile. She was turning thirteen on December 31 and was planning a party at home on December 29. She attended St. Maurice, the local parish school, and was in the seventh grade.

Conversely, Barbara Grimes, who was three inches shorter than her younger sister, was quieter. She was a sophomore at the local public high school, having finished grade school at the parish school. Barbara had a part time job at a local furniture store, and helped contribute to the family's finances.

The two sisters were very close, and were often seen walking hand in hand.

On The Day In Question:

On December 28th, 1956, both girls were very excited. Like many teenage girls, they were both huge fans of Elvis Presley, and were members of his fan club. His debut film, *Love Me Tender,* had finished its downtown run and was opening at their local theatre. By that time they had already seen the film ten times, but were planning on going again that night.

The girls managed to convince their mother to allow them to go out, despite the fact that one of the girls had been unwell and the weather was reported to turn bad that night. However, she eventually relented, giving the girls $2.50, instructing them to put aside 50c for carfare home.

We don't know how the girls travelled to the theatre, but we do know that once there they met up with a friend of Patricia's named Dorothy Weinert, along with her own younger sister. That night the show was a double feature, and the Weinert girls left during the break between the two shows. They saw both Grimes girls waiting in line for popcorn. The girls were in good spirits, and nothing seemed to be out of place or unusual.

The Grimes sisters had decided to stay for the second show, and their mother expected them home around 11:45PM. However, they did not arrive. When they were still not home at midnight, Loretta Grimes asked their older brother and sister to wait for them together at the bus stop. They waited for three buses and then returned home to tell their mother the girls had not arrived. At 2:15AM, Patricia and Barbara Grimes were reported as missing.

Investigation:

At first, it was believed that the girls had simply run away, perhaps even to Nashville to see Elvis Presley himself in concert. The star even issued a statement of his own, telling the girls that if they were good fans, they would "…go home and ease your mother's worries."

Multiple sightings of both girls were reported. Some included seeing both girls board a bus after the movie, heading into the city, apparently alighting from the bus around 11:05PM only half way to their house.

Two teenage boys reported the girls walking through the neighborhood around 11:30PM, and a security guard reported being asked for directions by two girls matching the Grimes sister's descriptions near Central Park and Lawrence Avenues on the morning of December 29th.

The sightings continued. A classmate reported she passed them walking with two other unidentified girls in the street. Others reported that they were drunk in the street on December 30th, at a location more than five miles from the theatre. A hotel clerk also said that the girls checked into his hotel on the same day.

As December turned to January, the girls were still missing, and the sighting reports continued. Another report of them on a bus came in on January 1st. A lady reported picking them up from a bus station in Nashville and taking them to an agency to look for work. A clerk there confirmed the story, saying the girls used the surname Grimes.

Finally, on January 13th a friend of the sisters, Sandra Tollstan, received two telephone calls around midnight. At first, there was nobody there when she answered, but during the second call approximately fifteen minutes later, when Tollstan's mother Anne, answered the phone, she heard a frightened voice asking for Sandra. The caller had hung up by the time she fetched her daughter but Ann Tollstan was convinced that the voice on the other end belonged to Patricia Grimes.

The sightings perhaps may have continued to go on into February, were it not for a gruesome discovery on January 22nd, 1957. A man named Leonard Prescott had been driving along German Church Road, on his way to a grocery store, when he noticed what he thought were two mannequins laying on the side of the road.

Prescott returned home to pick up his wife, and they both then traveled back to the scene. What they thought were mannequins turned out to be the naked bodies of two girls. Their grisly find was reported to police at 1:30PM.

The bodies were identified as being those of the missing Grimes girls. Both naked, Barbara was laying face down on the bottom, with Patricia's body perpendicular on top and facing up. Investigators now believed that despite the numerous reported sightings, the girls had been killed on the day they disappeared, and the heavy snow had hidden the evidence until now.

Examination of their stomach contents estimated their time of death to be within five hours of when they had last been seen at the theatre. One person however disagreed. Harry Glos, a chief investigator with the coroner's office, believes that a thin layer of ice found on the bodies could not have formed before January 7th, when the snowfalls were heavy enough to react with their warm bodies and form the ice layer.

Scavenging animals had damaged both girls' faces, but there were no fatal wounds on either girl. Nor had they been drugged or poisoned. Barbara's body had three puncture wounds on her chest, and it was also discovered that she had likely had sex shortly before her death. However, there was no evidence to suggest it was not consensual. Eventually, the official cause of death was ruled as shock from exposure.

There were several suspects in this case. The major one was a man named Edward Lee "Bennie" Bedwell, a twenty-one year old drifter from Tennessee. Illiterate, Bedwell worked as a dishwasher in a restaurant, and the owner claimed that he had approached the Grimes sisters when they visited the establishment on December 30th.

However, apart from the dissenting investigator Harry Glos, investigators believed that the girls were apparently already dead at this time. It's said that Bedwell had a passing resemblance to Elvis himself, and so was perhaps the restaurant owner seeing what she wanted to see?

However, whether or not they really met up with him, Bedwell signed a confession saying that he and another man were with the sisters from the 7th of January, and after drinking with them for seven days on 'skid row', they murdered both sisters by beating them to death after they refused sex.

He claimed that they had fed the girls hot dogs just before their deaths. He was charged with murder on January 27th, however he later recanted the confession, claiming it was coerced. By then, evidence from the autopsy revealed no trace of hotdogs in the girl's stomach contents.

The sister's mother also claimed they would never have engaged in such behavior. Finally, Bedwell had an alibi for the official time of death. He had been clocked in at work from 4:19PM on the 28th of December until 12:30AM the following morning.

Again, the sole dissenter was Harry Glos. He believed that the marks on the girl's bodies needed further investigation, and that those along with the sexual activity fit with Bedwell's explanation of their deaths. He claimed a conspiracy theory was involved, stating that parts of the crime were being covered up to protect the reputation of the victims and spare the family from the more lurid details.

After refusing to retract the allegations, Glos was fired from his position. It is worth nothing that as time has passed and others have examined the case files, there are now more people who share Glos's view.

There were other suspects. One was a seventeen year-old minor by the name of Max Fleig. He took a lie detector test voluntarily and failed, at which time he confessed that he kidnapped the sisters. However, it was at the time illegal to give a minor a polygraph test and so police were forced to let him go.

He was never charged with the girls' kidnapping and murder as no other evidence linking him was uncovered. However, a couple of years later Fleig was found guilty of murdering another young woman in an unrelated case.

Then there was the strange involvement of a fifty-three year old man named Walter Kranz. A blue- collar tradesman, Kranz called police on the 15th of January to report that he'd had a dream about the girls, and named a location where their bodies would be found. It turned out that the location was only one and a half miles from the true final resting place.

His explanation was that psychic powers ran in his family. However, after being interrogated multiple times by police, he was released without charge.

Finally, there is Silas Jayne. Unknown to police at the time of the Grime's sisters murder, it was revealed through the investigation into the disappearance of Helen Brach, discussed in *Murders Unsolved*, that he was connected to other murders of children in 1955. At the time of the Grime's sisters' murders, he owned stables in the same town where their bodies were found.

Current Status:
The funeral for both girls was held on January 28th, 1957, and was donated by a local funeral home. A mass was also held at the grade school. Many people attended the funeral, including the Mayor of Chicago. The sisters were then buried in the Catholic cemetery.

After the girl's death, their mother volunteered for many years at a prison located not far from where their bodies were found. Perhaps she hoped that she might learn something that would lead to the discovery of the person responsible for Patricia and Barbara's deaths.

Other theories of the case have come forward in more recent times, including a possible link between the murder of the sisters and that of a fifteen year-old girl named Bonnie Leigh Scott around a year later.

Shortly after Scott's body was recovered, the man ultimately found responsible for that crime, named Charles Melquist, allegedly called Loretta Grimes and boasted that he had also been the one to kill her girls.

Loretta Grimes claims that the voice matched an obscene phone call she received regarding the girl's disappearance originally, but Melquist was never charged with the crime. After being imprisoned for eleven years for Scott's murder, he was released and went on to marry and have two children.

Lynn Harper: Still Waiting For Justice

Victim: Lynn Harper
Date: June 9th, 1959
Location: Clinton, Ontario
Suspect: Steve Truscott

Backstory:
Cheryl "Lynn" Harper was born on August 31st, 1946. She lived in Moncton, a city in New Brunswick, Canada, along with her parents Leslie and Shirley Harper, and her younger brother, Jeffery. She also had an older brother named Barry, who lived in Ohio.

In 1940, her father (who had previously been a teacher) joined the military, and the family moved to an air force base near Clinton, Ontario.

As well as school, Harper attended Girl Guides, bible class, and Sunday School. She is reported as being a brash and determined girl, and could be headstrong.

On The Day In Question:
On June 9th, 1959, Harper attended school as usual. She went to school at Air Vice Marshal Hugh Campbell School, which was on the northern side of the base. Along with her other classmates in a combined 7th and 8th grade class, she had a classmate named Steven Truscott.

Early in the evening of that day, it's known that Truscott and Harper rode together on his bike traveling from school along County Road. What happened next has been in debate ever since. What we do know is that Harper disappeared on that bike ride, and on the next day her body was found by police lying inside a wooded grove. She had been raped and murdered.

Investigation:

From the beginning of the investigation, Truscott was a suspect. Harper's parents reported her missing at 11:20PM on June 9th, and on the morning of June 10th, Truscott was interviewed at his school, in a police cruiser.

Truscott's story never changed. He said that he left Harper on the side of the road at an intersection, unharmed. As he rode away, he glanced back and saw her getting into a car he did not recognize.

On the evening of June 12th, Truscott was arrested and very early the following day he was officially charged with first-degree murder. Despite being only fourteen years old, he was tried as an adult under the Juvenile Delinquents Act. An appeal against that order was denied.

Truscott's trial commenced on September 16th, with very little evidence. Not only was there little to go on, the evidence was all purely circumstantial, and relied heavily on a very narrow time of death of just fifteen minutes.

With modern forensics we now know that pinpointing time of death to that degree was impossible in this case. Despite this, on September 30th, 1959, the jury returned a verdict of guilty. As per the law at the time, despite the jury recommending mercy, Truscott was sentenced to hang.

The case was over, or so it was thought.

On the January 21st, 1960, Truscott's lawyer appealed his conviction in the Court of Appeals, and it was dismissed. However, the government did immediately commute his death sentence to life in prison. Back then, there was no automatic right of appeal, and an application for Leave to Appeal Further was denied on February 24th.

A book released in 1966 had already started to turn popular opinion, and by April the Canadian Government referred the case to the Supreme Court. Five days of evidence were heard in 1966, and submissions were included in January of 1967. A British pathology professor also reviewed the forensic evidence.

The forensic analysis was presented to the court on May 4th, 1967, and on the same day Truscott testified, telling his story to the court for the first time. He had not testified in the original trial. However, the Supreme Court had then ruled that a new trial should not be granted, and Truscott was returned to prison.

Until his sentence was commuted, Truscott had been held at the adult Huron Prison. After the commutation, he was moved to another prison for assessment and then eventually transferred to Ontario Training School for Boys. He was moved again to Collins Bay Penitentiary in 1963 when he turned eighteen, and by 1967 to the Farm Annex of the same prison due to his spotless record while incarcerated.

He remained there for another two years, and on October 21st, 1969, Truscott was released on parole. At this time he was only twenty-four years old and had already been in prison for ten years.

He lived with his parole officer for a short while, and was then resettled under an alias. He married and had three children. In November of 1974, since he had been employed and free from any criminal activity since his release, he was relieved of parole conditions.

That might have been the end of it. However, perhaps because of his age and also some of the questionable evidence at his trial, the case of his conviction for Harper's murder has always had a large public appeal.

Current Status:

Interest was again reignited in the case with the release of another book in 2000, along with a television program. An appeal was lodged again on November 28th, 2001, and on January 24th, 2002 the government appointed a retired Quebec Justice to review the case.

Harper's body was exhumed to attempt to collect DNA evidence, but none was found. However, we now know that the insect evidence used to determine Hartley's time of death was flawed, and she could have died as late as the next day.

It was also discovered that another witness had corroborated seeing Truscott riding his bike over a bridge. At trial, two other boys confirmed that testimony, but they had been discredited as liars in the first trial.

The new witness, Karen Daum, had never been called. The rules surrounding criminal court trials were very different in the 1950's and today many say that we would not even call them fair trials.

There was now also doubt as to whether the most likely perpetrator of such a horrific sexual crime was a fourteen year-old boy who, prior to being charged with Harper's murder, had no other record of any criminal offence. Police had been focused on Truscott from the very beginning. Had they then neglected to consider other possibilities?

A new appeal was again launched in January of 2007. Already a popular case, it is also notable for the fact that it was the first time cameras were allowed into the hearing. Arguments for and against were heard over a ten-day period, and then on August 28th, 2007, forty-eight years after he was originally convicted, Truscott was officially acquitted of the crime.

Steve Truscott received $6.5 million in compensation from the Ontario government. The case continues to attract attention, and most recently was the inspiration for a play in 2008, called *Innocence Lost*.

Harper's family has never supported Truscott's acquittal. Now that he has been cleared of the crime, officially it is once again unsolved.

The Walker Family: An Evil Obsession?

Victims: The Walker Family
Date: December 19th, 1959
Location: Palmer Ranch, near Osprey, Florida
Suspects: Curtis McCall, Stanley Mauck, Wilbur Tooker, Elbert Walker, Perry Smith and Dick Hickock

Backstory:
The Walker family was a family of four, living in Osprey, Florida. The family members included Cliff (25), Christine (24), and their two children Jimmie (3), and Debbie (23 months). They had been married for five years, and although the family lived a simple life, it was a happy one.

Cliff worked as a ranch hand for the Palmer family. Christine was occasionally lonely living on the ranch, but her husband loved his job and the children were happy, and so she was known for keeping these feelings to herself. They had family and friends in Arcadia and visited often.

However, there were rumors that even after marriage, Christine perhaps enjoyed the attention of other men a bit too much. She was described as being 'well-built' and often dressed herself in clothing that showed off her figure.

On The Day In Question:
The family had a busy Saturday planned on December 19th, 1959. First, the family headed into the local store to pick up groceries. Christine told the store's owner that she was mad at her husband as he had gotten himself into a fight, but she refused to say any more about it.

She had also told Cliff's mother the previous day that "Your son liked to got killed yesterday", but had not revealed any more as Cliff had walked in the room.

The family test drove two cars, and visited a hardware shop for food, drink, and cigarettes for Cliff, a vice he never went without.

The family then visited family friends, Don and Lucy McLeod and their two children, who also lived on an outpost on the ranch. Cliff and Don went on a quick hunting trip while the women watched the children and chatted.

When they were ready to go home, they loaded up a jeep with cattle feed that Cliff had to take back to his house, and they left. The children wanted to ride in the jeep, and so Christine drove the family car home alone, leaving about fifteen minutes before her husband.

It was about a twenty-minute drive back to their house on the ranch. She arrived around 4PM. Later, investigators determined that the Walker's car was not parked in its usual place. Police theorized that someone else was parked there first, someone that Christine must have known for her to get out of the car and go inside. Her purse was inside and the groceries were put away. She had gone into the house voluntarily.

Perhaps the visitor had been a man who fancied Christine, and decided that having caught her alone, he could try to make a move on her. When police examined her body later, they would discover that Christine had been punched in the face, she had been raped and then shot.

The first wound was only superficial, but the second was to her head and killed her. A quilt was laid over the now bloody bed, and her body was cleaned with another quilt, before being dragged to the living room.

Cliff and the children arrived home no later than 4:35PM, having stopped to fill the jeep's tires on the way. There was a loaded rifle in the back of the jeep, but he must have had no idea what awaited him at his home, and left it in the back of the vehicle.

As he stepped through the front door, Cliff was also shot, the first bullet meeting its mark, and he dropped where he stood. The children were now alone and defenseless.

Perhaps the killer paused when he realized that really, they were just babies and perhaps not. We will never know. Jimmie, just three years old, was shot three times before he died, lying next to his father.

The killer then shot baby Debbie in the head, but the first shot didn't kill her, and he was out of bullets. Picking her up, she dripped a trail of blood to the bathroom as he carried her. The drain was blocked with a sock, and the killer drowned the baby in the bath.

Early the next morning, before the sun was up, Don McLeod set out to the Walker's house on the ranch. Don and Cliff had spotted wild hogs when out digging a fire line a couple of days earlier, and they wanted to catch them when they were returning from foraging all night. They had planned an early hunting trip for that morning.

The two men had often hunted together before, and each time, despite the early start, Cliff was always ready and waiting, with a pot of hot coffee to share. This morning however, the house was dark and quiet when Don arrived. For once he had caught his friend asleep!

At first he wondered if they had gone to visit his father in Arcadia. The man had been ill lately, and perhaps they had gotten some bad news late at night. However, he believed that Cliff would still have let him know he couldn't make their hunting trip.

He found both the front and back doors locked, and when peering through the windows revealed nothing except a flickering light, he started to worry. Using his pocketknife, he cut a hole in the screen door and then used the blade to pop the hook open. The interior door was unlocked, and he could then enter the house.

McLeod turned on the kitchen light, and it gave him just enough light to be able to see down into the house. The first thing he saw was Christine's bare feet. He worried that an old gas heater at the property had gone out and suffocated the family. When McLeod moved to look closer, he saw a scene that will likely haunt him for the rest of his life.

Christine still lay where she had been dragged into the living room doorway, Cliff lay on his back where he fell, and Jimmie was lying only a few inches from his father. Blood coated the entire scene. It was now obvious that it hadn't been a heater that had killed his friends.

Panicking that the killer could still be in the house, he tore outside, and remembering that his truck still had the horse trailer attached, decided to take the jeep. He noticed the feed was still loaded, and that the rifle sat in the cab.

McLeod first stopped at a payphone, but he didn't have any money, and so he drove to a nearby restaurant that was just opening. They didn't have a phone, but the owner gave him money to go back and use the payphone.

He drove back and called the Sarasota police. Initially he was told he had to call the county Sheriff, but he responded that he didn't have any more money for more calls and then said, "They're all dead."

Investigation:
There was little physical evidence found at the scene. Just a footprint made in blood that looked like it had come from a cowboy boot. Investigators also found a cellophane strip from a cigarette packet, a single fingerprint on the

bathroom faucet, and seven empty .22 caliber shells. The cigarettes were not the brand that Cliff smoked. That was it. No weapons were left at the scene.

Christine's clothes had been partially disturbed with her dress and slip pulled up to partly cover her face. She was however fully dressed. There were streaks of blood around Jimmie, indicating to investigators that the three year old had crawled to lay closer to his father after he had been shot.

The Sheriff's deputies were first on the scene, and were already examining the house and surrounding area for clues when the Sheriff arrived at dawn. Over the course of the investigation a State Attorney was present to oversee any discoveries, along with the Sheriff, and ballistics and fingerprint experts.

It was reported in the newspapers of the time that the officers struggled to deal with the tragedy and that they were visibly shaken with what they witnessed at the crime scene.

Sheriff Ross Boyer, himself only twenty years old at the time of the murders, was known to be particularly intolerant of any blood, and would occasionally pass out after attending the scene of an accident. However, on this morning he held his own and did what needed to be done.

He knew that the scope of the crime scene was larger than anything he or his deputies had ever dealt with before. With no official crime scene photographer, he relied on a photographer from a local newspaper to document the scene, and also allowed a reporter inside the house.

Police could not identify what type of gun had been used based only on the spent shells, but they believed that they would be able to match it should they find the murder weapon, due to a distinctive mark that had been left on the casings.

However, in a rural town where many families relied on guns for multiple purposes, this was easier said than done. Guns were routinely carried around for day-to-day activities, and many people owned one.

Friends of the family couldn't name anyone that would want to hurt them. They reported that Cliff did not drink or gamble. While he had had his debts, he had told friends that he expected to clear them all by Christmas.

Police believed that the killer was already in the house before anyone came home, and he laid in wait for Christine Walker. One has to wonder how he knew she would be coming home alone? The authorities also believe that the children were killed because they could identify the killer.

At three years old, Jimmie was apparently already an accomplished talker. Perhaps the killer was afraid he would reveal who murdered his parents if he was left alive. You still however have to wonder, why kill the baby?

The Sheriff's office had access to a polygraph machine, and it was immediately put to use interviewing anyone who had a connection to the family. The first to be interviewed was Don McLeod. He passed the test and was released. He then drove home to break the horrible news to his wife.

For Christine Walker's family, reminders of their daughter kept arriving even after her death. A letter that she had posted to her mother before she died arrived the next day. The family's possessions were then shipped to her mother's house, including the chest that had held Christine's most precious memento; her majorette uniform from high school.

She had never needed much encouragement to show it off, and had told anyone who would listen that she was saving it for when baby Debbie was older. However, it was now missing, removed from the chest, leaving only the plastic bag behind.

Also missing from the crime scene was the Walker's one wall decoration, their framed marriage certificate. The only other things that had been taken from the crime scene were Cliff's cigarettes and his pocketknife.

Investigators became increasingly convinced that the murders were committed by someone who intimately knew the family; enough to take only their most prized possessions as trophies. The leading theory was that the murderer was a man who was obsessed with Christine and had finally decided to approach her. When he was refused, his rage was triggered.

But then again, investigators wondered, had his advances been originally entirely unwelcome? A couple of Christine's friends told police that she had asked them about how you could terminate a pregnancy, and in that last year she had suffered two miscarriages. Investigators started to wonder if Christine had been in fact having an affair and had been trying to hide the evidence.

In the end, what convinced them that the family had been intimately acquainted with their killer were the deaths of the children. Sheriff Boyer was convinced that had he been a stranger, he would have left the children alive. After all, why would he have killed them if not for the fact they could identify him?

These days, we know that the murder of children does tragically happen, more often than one likes to think about. Despite the Sheriff's beliefs, it is not a foregone conclusion that the Walkers knew their killer.

Time went by, and no one was charged with the crime. And then, a couple of months afterwards women found bloody clothes in a shed located only one or two miles from the house. The clothes were identified as having belonged to Cliff and Christine Walker. Had the killer used the items to wipe himself of their blood?

Now, as well as men known to get a little rowdy or flirty when drunk, police widened their net to include any locals who had a history of violence against women. They still believed that the killer had to be intimately familiar with the local area to know about the location of the shed.

Sheriff Boyd assured the public that they would never give up trying to solve the case.

Time and again, promising leads would be discovered in the case, only to have them lead nowhere. Over time, a number of people were named as suspects, but nothing ever led to charges being made.

One suspect came from a statement given to police by the cousin of a man named Curtis McCall in 1963. He was convinced that McCall had been having an affair with Christine Walker, stating that he knew it as a fact.

McCall looked promising; he had been one of Christine's boyfriends in high school, though his cousin claimed they had never really broken up, despite Christine and Cliff marrying.

The cousin claimed that just two weeks before the murders, Christine had arrived at his mother's house looking for McCall, while her husband was away at a rodeo. McCall had a history of violence, attacking suspects of his own while arresting them in his capacity as a Florida Highway Patrol dispatcher. He was fired for the incident. Lastly, McCall owned a .22 caliber pistol.

McCall's cousin reported that since the murders McCall had grown increasingly withdrawn and edgy, often refusing to eat and becoming increasingly nervous. He was interviewed by police, but denied dating Christine at all.

He claimed that the one time he'd seen her before the murders, Cliff had also been present. He also claimed that he had sold the gun, but couldn't remember to whom. Investigators gave McCall a polygraph, but the results showed only that he was nervous.

Finally, after multiple tests, the only question that gave a definitive result was when he was asked if he was withholding information from police on the murders. According to the polygraph results, he was. It is not known where McCall now resides or what happened to him.

Another suspect was an electricity meter reader named Stanley Mauck. He seemed like a normal guy, chatting to families that he met along his route. However, Mauck hid a troubling secret. He had been under the care of a psychiatrist to treat an uncontrollable urge he had to kill his wife and children. Becoming increasingly desperate to solve the case, investigators had their eye on Mauck from early on.

He was already a suspect in a bizarre murder in Sarasota. The apartment where the crime occurred was on his meter route. When it was discovered that the Walker house was also on his route, he officially became a suspect. However, no evidence was ever found to link Mauck to either crime, and the other, known as the Mummy Murder, also remains unsolved.

Shortly after the Walker murders, Mauck suffered a complete breakdown and ended up receiving electric shock therapy. His wife came forward in 2005, stating that the Walker case nearly broke him, and he would often just walk the streets and cry.

Then there was a retired railway worker, who was thought by many to fit the perpetrator perfectly. Wilbur Tooker lived about a mile away from the Walkers, and had visited so often that he was now unwelcome. Christine Walker's mother told detectives that he made many unwelcome advances on Christine, and she was afraid of him.

Other witnesses came forward and told police that they had seen Tooker try to manhandle Christine, and try to kiss her or drag her into bed. Christine had finally told Cliff, who allegedly wanted to kill Tooker, but was talked out of it by a friend. Tooker was told to never come around to the house again.

Detectives traced Tooker's movements the day of the crime. He had eaten dinner with a friend in Sarasota between 5-7PM. This left him with no alibi for the time of the killings. After dinner he played violin in an orchestra performance at Bradenton High School.

Police asked other members of the orchestra if he behaved oddly that night, but they were told that he was such a poor player, you could not tell if he was having an off night from one day to another. Wilbur Tooker was never charged with the crimes and died in 1963.

Then there was Cliff's cousin Elbert Walker. He was very vocally upset at the funeral, and also fainted twice during the service. However, family members claimed he had been faking his distress. Walker was described as someone who was a bit wild and often got belligerent when drunk. They believed he had the personality of someone who would have carried on an affair with Christine, and the type to commit the crime.

His behavior surrounding the day the murders were discovered was odd. He had been in town, claiming he'd come to discuss a party he was going to host with Cliff, but detectives stated that this was untrue. Witnesses who saw him that day reported that he had bloodshot eyes and looked like he had "had a rough night".

He asked people where the family lived, strange in itself as he had visited often and knew how to get there. He was informed of the killings by one of the men he asked for directions to the house, but when he got to the house itself, acted as if he was hearing the news for the first time all over again.

Perhaps most telling, Elbert Walker allegedly told his girlfriend that Jimmie hadn't died immediately, and had crawled up to his daddy. That detail had never been released to the public. So how had Walker known?

However, Elbert Walker himself has always denied any involvement in the murders. He too passed a lie detector test. In modern times however that result has been called into question, with today's experts pointing out the unreliability of the results from older machines.

Technology has improved, and the operators are also now extensively trained, compared with perhaps the ten minutes from the salesman in the 1950's. Walker was tested again in 1987, with a new machine, an expert operator, and also present was an expert on the Walker case. He passed again.

Current Status:
Then, there came the lead that many thought would finally break the case wide open. It involved one of the most famous murders of the twentieth century, named the Cutter Murders after the name of the victims.

In November of 1959, two men broke into a ranch house that was rumored to have thousands of dollars hidden away inside by the farmer who lived there. When nothing was found, the two men killed not only the farmer, but his wife and both their children. The two men, named Perry Smith and Dick Hickock, were arrested for the murders in Las Vegas on December 30th, 1959.

There were incredible similarities in the Cutter and Walker family murders, both in their timing, only one month apart, and both being family massacres. A bloody cowboy boot footprint had also been found at the scene of both murders, and the men had been near Sarasota, only a few hours from the Walker's house, when the family was murdered. However, the pair denied any involvement in the murders of the Walker family, and a polygraph test agreed with them.

Investigators however were not convinced. They ran newspaper stories asking that anyone who might have seen them in the area in the last two months to contact Sheriff Boyer. Many calls confirmed that the two men were in Sarasota between December 16th and 20th, and the Walkers had been murdered on the 19th.

In the end, there was simply not any evidence to tie them to the crime. Fingerprint evidence didn't match, and when their movements were more closely tracked, investigators could not place them close enough to the scene of the crime. The pair was hanged for the Cutter murders in 1965.

That was however not the end of it. In December of 2012, the bodies of Perry Smith and Dick Hickock were exhumed and their DNA extracted. It was tested against semen found on Christine Walker's body from the rape. As current cases took priority, it was not until August of 2013 that the results were released; no match was found.

However, due to the degradation of the samples over the decades, investigators have said that this result can neither prove nor disprove any involvement by the two men in the death of the Walker family. The investigation is back where it started.

Sheriff Boyd, along with his deputies, often spoke of solving the case before they retired. Then, it changed simply to hope that it would be solved before they died. Today, more than fifty years since the tragic deaths in Osprey that day, the case remains open.

Mary Meyer: The Socialite Who Loved JFK

Victim: Mary Pinchot Meyer
Date: October 1964
Location: Georgetown, Washing D.C.
Suspect: Raymond Crump

Backstory:
Mary Meyer was born Mary Pinchot on October 14th, 1920 to parents Amos and Ruth Pinchot. Mary, her sister Antoinette and half siblings Rosamund and Gifford, were raised in wealth and status.

As she grew up, Meyer's family was already involved in politics, including her uncle Gifford Pinchot, who had twice been the Governor of Pennsylvania. As an American socialite she was involved deeply in the Washington D.C. political scene.

Pinchot attended Vassar College and first met John F. Kennedy in 1938 at a dance while on a date with another man.

Pinchot married Cord Meyer in 1944. Cord Meyer was a veteran of the Marines and later involved in the CIA in covert operations against communism. They had three children together, and when Meyer became involved in the CIA, the family moved to Washington D.C. In 1955, tragedy struck the family when a car struck their son Michael, 9, and killed him. In 1958, Mary Meyer filed for divorce.

Friends of Meyer recall that her lifestyle changed after the divorce and she became a 'well bred ingenue' having fun and getting into trouble. It was at this time that she became friends with Robert Kennedy.

In October of 1961, she visited John F. Kennedy at the Whitehouse, and they began an intimate relationship. As well as being friends with Jackie Kennedy, Meyer was also in bed with her husband, quite literally, as a known mistress of JFK.

On The Day In Question:
After her divorce, Meyer began painting again, and set up a converted garage at her home as a studio. On Monday October 12, 1964, Meyer finished her latest work.

Around noon, she decided to go for a walk, and traveled on foot along the Chesapeake and Ohio Canal towpath in Georgetown. A mechanic in the area, Henry Wiggins, reported hearing a woman cry-out, "Someone help me", and he then heard two shots from a gun.

When he ran to the scene, he saw a black man in a light jacket, dark slacks, and a cap standing over the body of a white woman. An Air Force Lieutenant, William Mitchell, also claimed to have passed both Meyer and the same suspect on the path.

Investigation:
When the police were called, they arrived quickly on the scene and the victim was identified as Mary Meyer. She had two bullet wounds, one in her head and one in her chest. A forensic investigator would later determine that the shots had been taken at close range.

Just minutes later, the police discovered an African American man near the scene of the crime. He was soaking wet and his clothing was disheveled. He was arrested, despite not having a gun on or near his person. The man's name was Raymond Crump.

Crump claimed that his fishing rod had fallen in the river and he had gone into the river to find it. He then also told police that he had been drinking and fallen into the river while asleep.

However, a witness to the shooting positively identified him as the man who had been standing over Meyer's body. On investigation, police found Crump's jacket and cap in the river, and his fishing rod at home in his closet.

The murder weapon was not recovered at the scene, and has never been found.

Crump was tried for the murder, but was acquitted on all charges. His defense lawyer demonstrated to the court that there were other exists from the path that had not been sealed by police, and they were also able to get Wiggins to state that he could not positively identify the man he had seen on the day as Crump.

There were also arguments based on his alleged height when compared to Lieutenant Mitchell's testimony. After eleven hours, the jury was deadlocked but eventually found Crump not guilty.

Interestingly, it had been ruled that Meyer's private life could not be discussed in the courtroom. Any past that the victim had with JKF was also kept from Crump's defense lawyer, who recalls he was unable to find out anything about her at all.

With Crump's acquittal, the murder remains officially unsolved.

Current Status:
In 1998, journalist Nina Burleigh released a book about Meyer. Titled *A Very Private Woman* it investigates the theories surrounding Meyer's death.

One prominent theory is that Meyer was killed by the same party or parties that assassinated John F. Kennedy. Another writer named C. David Heymann claims that this theory was substantiated to him by Cord Meyer on his deathbed. Some believe that the CIA was involved in both murders.

There are almost endless theories as to who assassinated President Kennedy. Was Meyer close enough to him to be taken out by the same people? Since her death rumors have surfaced that she took drugs with Kennedy, including LSD (then legal in the US) and marijuana, and she had influenced Kennedy's opinions on nuclear disarmament and Cuba.

Perhaps some thought her influence over Kennedy needed to be removed. On the other hand, perhaps because of her husband's connections, she knew too much about the murder of Kennedy herself.

The other major theory speaks to larger issues within the community of that era as a whole. It suggests that Crump, driven by oppression and a segregated city, took action against Meyer as a representative of the white man's oppression and racism against blacks.

Is it possible that Crump woke up one day, went for a walk in the city, and then engaged in the unplanned murder of a white woman, simply over simmering feelings of racism and injustice?

After being acquitted of Meyer's murder, Crump lived a life of crime. He was arrested twenty-two times in Washington D.C. over his life, for crimes including assault, arson, and rape. Despite his acquittal, with hindsight his innocence in Meyer's death does not look so assured.

Sam Giancana: The Mobster's Last Supper

Victim: Sam Giancana
Date: 1975
Location: Oak Park, Illinois
Suspects: Anthony Accardo, Angelo LaPietra, Joseph J. Auippa , other mob members

Backstory:
Sam Giancana was born on Chicago's West Side. His parents were Sicilian immigrants, and named him Salvatore Giangana. When Giancana was growing up, his family owned a pushcart, and then later an Italian ice shop. The shop ended up being firebombed by rivals of Giancana.

When he was a teen, Giancana was involved in a gang called The 42s. The group allegedly was involved in low-level jobs for members of the Chicago Mafia, which at the time was led by Al Capone. After this, Giancana received a job as a driver in the organization. His first arrest was in 1925 for auto theft, but he avoided jail time.

Giancana rose quickly through the organization, and by the time he was twenty years old he was already the major suspect in three different murder investigations. However, he never went to trial for any of the crimes.

Giancana married Angeline DeTolve in 1933, and over time, the couple would have three daughters. He continued to climb the ranks of the mob, and in 1939 he served his first jail term for the illegal manufacture of whiskey.

Prison obviously did not reform him, as when he was released Giancana took over Chicago's illegal lottery operation. He was allegedly involved in a number of brutal events to take control of the racket, including kidnapping and murder. It increased the income of the mob by millions a year.

DeTolve died in 1954, leaving Giancana as a widower with three daughters to raise. He would never marry again.

As part of an interview for service during World War II, Giancana was given a psychological interview. The psychologist found him to have a psychopathic personality and strong antisocial behaviors.

By 1950, Anthony Accardo retired as the leader of the Chicago mob, and Giancana stepped up. With Giancana as their leader, the mob's influence grew, and he came under the notice of the FBI. The FBI would plant a bug in the Armory Lounge (which Giancana used as his headquarters) in 1959, and would continue to listen in on him for the next six years.

Giancana continued to be a powerful force in Chicago's mob scene, and even had ties to such famous families as the Kennedys. Although he never remarried, he is rumored to have had several famous lovers. There were also rumors that Giancana was involved in a ballot-stuffing scheme that helped John F. Kennedy's 1960 election.

Giancana was on trial for his refusal to testify to a grand jury in relation to organized crime in 1965. As a result, he was given a year and a half's jail term. When he was released, Giancana traveled to Mexico, and continued to live there until 1974.

That year, Giancana was extradited to testify to a second grand jury. This time, he was given immunity and although he testified four separate times, nothing he provided was ever useful.

On The Day In Question:
After his original grand jury testimony, Giancana was called to testify again, this time to a senate committee that

was looking into any involvement of the Mafia in a plot by the CIA to assassinate Fidel Castro.

Before Giancana was supposed to appear before the committee, he had gall bladder surgery in Houston, Texas. He then flew home to Oak Park to recuperate. On June 19th, two days after returning home, he was shot and killed. He took one shot in the back of the head and then several more in the chin.

Investigation:
The bullets from the murder weapon were identified as being from a .22 caliber pistol. Police believe that the weapon was also fitted with a silencer.

Police believe that Giancana may have been expecting company that night. He was killed while cooking sausages and peppers. Due to his health, he was unable to eat spicy food. Was Giancana murdered by someone he knew well enough to invite to dinner?

There were many possible suspects. Anyone from a rival mafia, to the CIA, or one of multiple former girlfriends could have been guilty of the murder. However, no one has ever been arrested or charged with the crime.

The primary theory among law enforcement is that Giancana was killed by a rival. Sources have reported that the hit could have been sanctioned only by Joseph J. Auippa and Anthony J. Accardo, the Chicago Outfit's 'bosses of the bosses'. There is no evidence to suggest who actually pulled the trigger.

Current Status:
In the 2000's, a hit man named Nicholas Calabrese told the FBI that he knew that Tony Accardo was involved in the killing. He also named Angelo LaPietra (another Chicago mobster) as the man who disposed of the gun.

Predictably, the CIA has denied any involvement or prior knowledge of the hit.

Friends and colleagues of Giancana are convinced that he knew his killer, saying that he was far too careful to open the door to just anyone. One is quoted as saying that Giancana 'should've remembered what happened to Bugsy Siegel'.

Giancana continues to be featured in pop culture, in everything from fiction books, rap music, films and TV miniseries. One of his daughters released a book named *Mafia Princess*. It has since been adapted into a made for TV movie in 1986. Tony Curtis played the role of Giancana.

To this day Giancana's murder remains unsolved.

Tammy Vincent: Lost For Thirty Years

Victim: Tammy Vincent
Dates: August-September 1979
Locations: Seattle, Washington and San Francisco, California
Suspect: An unidentified white male

Backstory:
The story of Tammy Vincent spans many decades. Originally going missing in the summer of 1979, it would be nearly thirty years before she could be officially laid to rest.

Born in 1962, Vincent grew up on a farm. Her sister described her as being adventurous and fun. However, as she grew up, Vincent often fought with her parents. When she was sixteen, she moved to live in a foster home after the conflict with the family became too much. By the time she was seventeen, she had run away from the foster home.

The conflict with her family is believed to have played a part in why she decided to leave. There is evidence that she turned to prostitution as a way to survive after running away. She had been arrested when found in an apartment believed to be hiding girls and women working as prostitutes.

She was flown home, but she ran away before she could be returned to the custody of the Department of Social and Health Services (DSHS).

On The Day In Question:
Vincent visited her family for the last time in the summer of 1979, arriving in a car along with another unidentified person. Her family has since mentioned that she seemed different, speaking only briefly before leaving, never even leaving the car. However, they will not share what she

actually said. Her family denies any knowledge of what Vincent had been involved in.

Later in the same summer, Vincent's sister, Sandy, reports that she was contacted by Vincent, saying that she wanted to come home. She reports that Vincent was scared and 'knew her life was in danger'. That was the last time anyone would hear from her.

Investigation:
Investigation into Vincent's disappearance found a witness who placed her in Seattle on September 10th, 1979. They reported that they had seen Vincent entering a silver Lincoln Continental. Detectives traced the car and found it belonged to a suspect in the prostitution investigation in which Vincent had been involved.

As part of the trial, a judge signed an order of protection, identifying Vincent as a material witness. She was ordered to testify. The case was against 5 men, and they were charged with forcing both girls and women into prostitution. However, Vincent never testified. Instead, she disappeared.

When they did not hear from her, Vincent's family would periodically try to find information on her location. They thought that she might have been a victim of the Green River Killer; a serial killer we now know was responsible for at least forty-eight different murders. They contacted King County's Green River Task Force, who added Vincent to their list of missing women to investigate.

Despite the investigations, Vincent had simply disappeared, and that was the end of the case for nearly thirty years.

Current Status:
In 2002, the body of an unidentified murder victim was exhumed for further investigation in an attempt to identify

her. A composite image was created from her skull but the victim was not identified.

In 2003, Vincent's family was contacted by King County. A detective working on a task force wanted a DNA sample of a family member, something that was done as routine. Vincent's sister Sandy provided the sample.

The DNA was listed in a brand new national DNA registry that had been started at the University of North Texas. The university housed the Center for Human Identification, which stored information and tests remains for both crime labs and non-criminal cases.

Meanwhile, unbeknownst to the Vincent family, a detective from Marin County was looking at cold murder cases. He had re-opened a case from 1979, where a girl was found stabbed over forty times with an ice pick.

She had then been doused in acetone and set on fire. Finally, as she tried to run to escape, she had been shot in the head. Her death had been brutal, and no one had ever identified who she was.

Examining the old files, investigators found a clerk from a Woolworth's store in San Francisco who 'vividly recalled' a man wearing a white leisure suit coming into the store in the summer of 1979. With him was a girl who matched Vincent's description. It stuck in her mind because the man bought paint, acetone, and an ice pick.

Once they made the possible connection, detectives then went to find any physical evidence that still remained in the case. It had been moved through multiple different evidence lockers over the years, but they eventually found it. A single hair remained intact.

In 2005, they sent the hair to the California Department of Justice. The hair was compared to the database at the

University of North Texas in December of 2006. Just a few months later, in February of 2007, the results came back. They had a hit.

DNA was declared a match to the DNA that Sandy Vincent had supplied nearly four years earlier. Twenty-eight years later, Tammy Vincent was found.

Police broke the news to Vincent's family, and on August 10th, 2007, Vincent's remains were returned to them. She had been cremated and the remains were buried at a small ceremony attended by family members and friends.

Despite her identification, Vincent's murder remains unsolved. Marin County detective Steve Nash continues to work on the case.

Ken McElroy: The Town Bully

Victim: Ken McElroy
Date: 1981
Location: Skidmore, Missouri
Suspect: Del Clement

Backstory:
Ken McElroy was born on June 1st, 1934. He was from a large family, being the second youngest of sixteen children. Growing up, money was scarce. His parents were migrants and made a living as tenant farmers. They lived in Kansas and the Ozarks, before finally settling outside of a town called Skidmore in Missouri.

McElroy dropped out of school when he was fifteen years old and in the eighth grade, and he quickly established a reputation that was not entirely positive. He was known around town as a hunter, cattle rustler, and also a thief and womanizer.

He was suspected to be involved in many crimes that spanned over two decades, and although charges were brought against him more than twenty times, he was never convicted. It was thought that witnesses often failed to testify because they were intimated by McElroy.

Over his lifetime, McElroy fathered more than ten children with different women. His last wife, Trena McCloud, was only twelve when he first met her. By the time she was fourteen, McCloud was pregnant. She dropped out of school and moved in with McElroy and another woman, Alice Wood.

Just sixteen days after McCloud gave birth, both she and Wood left McElroy's home and went to McCloud's mother and stepfather's house. It is reported that when McElroy tracked them down, he dragged both women back home, and then killed the McCloud family dog and set their house on fire.

In June of 1973, he was indicted for arson, assault and statutory rape of McCloud. He was arraigned but gained release on $2,500 bail. Both McCloud and her baby were placed in foster care, and McElroy could be seen standing around outside the foster home for hours.

He also told the foster family that he would trade 'girl for girl', telling them he knew where their own biological daughter went to school, and what bus she took to get there. Additional charges were then filed against McElroy.

McElroy then decided to marry McCloud, so that she could not testify against him. However, given her age parental permission was required. To gain it, he threatened to burn down their house again. Permission was granted, and without the ability to use McCloud's testimony, he again escaped conviction.

Again in 1976, a Skidmore farmer accused McElroy of shooting him twice after the farmer challenged him for shooting weapons on the farmer's property. McElroy was charged with assault with intent to kill. A court date was not forthcoming for some time, and during this period the farmer reported that he had spotted McElroy parked outside his house more than one hundred times.

Finally, in court, the farmer was forced to admit his own conviction for a petty crime from more than thirty years ago, under questioning by McElroy's attorney. On this basis, McElroy was acquitted.

Meanwhile, his behavior did not seem to change. In 1980, he was charged with attempted murder. One of his children had gotten into an argument with a store clerk over the child allegedly stealing candy. In response, McElroy began stalking the family, and then threatened the storeowner with a shotgun.

During the incident, the storeowner was shot in the neck. Again, McElroy was freed on bail, and while on bail was overheard to make graphic threats towards his victim in public. Perhaps enough was finally enough and the local citizens approached the Sheriff to see what could be done to prevent McElroy harming anyone else. The Sheriff suggested they form a neighborhood watch.

On The Day In Question:
In the case of the shooting of the store owner, for the first time McElroy was found guilty. However he would not be found guilty of attempted murder, but of second-degree assault.

The judge set a maximum sentence of only two years, and McElroy was released on a bond pending appeal. Later, McElroy appeared in town carrying his gun and was rearrested, but was then released again.

On July 10, 1981, a hearing in relation to the case was once again delayed. In response, the townspeople met at a local hall with the Sheriff to discuss how they could protect themselves. Word of the meeting got back to McElroy, who was drinking in a local tavern with McCloud.

The Sheriff told the assembled crowd not to directly engage with McElroy, and he then left the scene. Once this happened, the townspeople instead gathered en masse at the tavern, and the bar was soon completely filled.

McElroy finished his drinks, purchased a six-pack of beer to take with him, and then left and returned to his vehicle. While he was still sitting behind the wheel, he was shot and hit twice, by two different guns.

Despite there being forty-six potential witnesses at the time of the crime, only McCloud was willing to name a gunman. Everyone else present denied knowing anything about the crime or who may have fired the fatal shots. Neither did anyone call emergency services. McElroy died in his truck.

Investigation:
No one has ever been named formally as a suspect or charged in the murder of McElroy. The District Attorney declined to press charges against anyone. A federal investigation took place, but no charges were laid as a result of their findings either.

Current Status:
Over thirty years have passed since McElroy's death. McElroy's lawyer's widow has told the media that she believes there was always enough evidence to take the case of McElroy's murder to trial, but that it was refused. She says that the town 'got away with murder'.

However, the police chief who oversaw the investigation disagrees. He reports that the town prosecutor was actually keen to bring the case to trial, but investigators could never secure enough evidence to win the case.

McCloud remarried and moved to Lebanon, Missouri. In 1984, she filed a wrongful death suit against the town, the Sheriff, the Mayor of Skidmore, and the man she accused of killing her husband, Del Clement. The suit was for $5 million.

No one ever admitted guilt, but the case was settled out of court for $17,600. She died of lung cancer in 2012. Her husband's murderer has never been identified.

Venus Xtravaganza: Killed For Her Gender?

Victim: Thomas Pellagatti aka Venus Xtravaganza
Date: December 21st, 1988
Location: New York City
Suspect: None

Backstory:
Thomas Pellagatti was born on May 22nd, 1966. Identifying early in life as a transsexual, she was cross-dressing from an early age. She then moved to New York as a way to avoid embarrassment for her family, taking on the name Venus in her early teen years.

Xtravaganza was part of the drag ball scene in New York in the 1980's. Born as a male but identifying as female, her stage name was Venus Xtravaganza. Her surname came from the House of Xtravaganza, one of the many 'houses' in New York that catered mostly to transgendered and gay youth. Often marginalized, the balls ran by the houses were a place where they could find acceptance and be who they were.

In the 1980's the AIDS epidemic was in crisis, and the balls were also a place where the gay and transexual community could escape the worries surrounding the condition.

On The Day In Question:
On December 25th, 1988, Xtravaganza's body was found under a bed in a hotel room in New York City. She had been strangled around December 21st and her body had lain there for four days before it was discovered. At the time of death, she was just twenty-three years old.

Investigation:
Xtravaganza worked as a prostitute while living in New York. She was pre-operative and saving up for sex reassignment surgery. While alive, she reported that some

of her clients became enraged when they discovered that she had male genitalia.

Incidents that made her fear for her life led her to leave the prostitution business and become an escort instead. Did one of her clients become so enraged as to murder her?

Current Status:
Venus Xtravaganza appeared in a documentary released in 1990 by Jennie Livingston called *Paris is Burning*.

No one has ever been arrested or charged in relation to Xtravaganza's murder. The crime remains unsolved.

Tammy Haas: Justice Denied in South Dakota

Victim: Tammy Haas
Date: September 17th, 1992
Location: Cedar County, Nebraska
Suspect: Erik Stukel

Backstory:
Tamara Ann Haas was born on April 13, 1973. She lived with her parents in Yankton, South Dakota, a medium sized city on the border between South Dakota and Nebraska. Tammy was a nineteen-year-old high school graduate from Yankton, South Dakota.

Her friends describe her as a beautiful young girl, who was also happy and cheerful. She played alto saxophone in the school band, and had also been involved in local dance productions since she was three years old. As a senior, she had been selected as homecoming royalty.

On The Day In Question:
On Thursday September 17th, 1992, Haas attended a homecoming party in Nebraska, near her hometown. She was going to the party with a date, Erik Stukel.

Over eighty people attended the party. Although the pair had to travel across the Missouri River, it was held on a family farm only eight miles from Yankton. Witnesses recall seeing Haas at the party, and walking towards Stukel's car around 11:00pm. After that, she disappeared.

No one saw or heard from Haas for almost a week, until a local who was looking for golf balls in a ravine stumbled across her body. The site of the discovery was only one mile from the farm where the party had been held.

Investigation:
After examining her body, which was found half-naked, investigators determined that Haas had been murdered

and then dumped in the ravine at most only half an hour after her death. Stomach contents placed time of death no later than 12:30pm on the night of the homecoming party.

An autopsy revealed that Haas had been viciously hit, likely tackled. However, cause of death could not be conclusively determined. Despite this, other evidence found at the crime scene led investigators to report her death was consistent with foul play.

The obvious suspect was Erik Stukel. Investigators found that he arrived at his parent's restaurant around 3:00-4:00am on the early morning of September 18th. He was drunk and severely impaired, and told one of his friends that 'I think I killed a girl'.

The friend however dismissed this as nothing more than drunken ramblings. This lasted until Haas' body was found, and then the friend went to the police.

When questioned by police, Stukel said that he had been with Haas at his house until 1:00am, at which time she left, traveling on foot. Stukel's sister confirmed she had seen Haas in a bathroom at their house around 1:00am.

However, the coroner's time of death had Haas already dead at this time. During a polygraph test, Stukel was asked if he killed Haas. He denied any involvement, but the polygraph results failed him on that question.

An investigation of Stukel's truck also found fibers that placed Haas inside the truck. Not a surprise since they went to the dance together. However, no motive was discovered and Stukel has never been formally charged with Haas' murder.

The case continues to attract attention, with many in her hometown calling for justice for Tammy Haas.

Current Status:
In 1995, Stukel was arrested for manslaughter in the case of Tammy Haas. At trial, the testimony of the friend where Stukel admitted killing a girl was stricken from the record.

Stukel was released on a $5,000 bond, and after thirteen hours of deliberation, the jury acquitted him. Officially, Haas' murder therefore remains unsolved.

Despite his acquittal, some of Haas' family and friends believe that Stukel knows exactly what happened to Haas that September night.

Chris Trickle: A Complete Mystery

Victim: Chris Trickle
Date: February 9th, 1997
Location: Las Vegas, Nevada
Suspect: None

Backstory:
Chris Trickle was born on May 30th, 1973 to Chuck and Barbara Trickle. He was the nephew of NASCAR driver Dick Trickle, and as he grew up, he followed in his footsteps.

During his childhood, Trickle raced motorcycles, and by the time he was fifteen he had two track championships. As a teen, he drove in a national touring series.

In 1990, Trickle changed from bikes to stock cars, and in 1992 was named Rookie of the Year. By 1996, he was competing exclusively in the Southwest Series, where he won one race and finished in the top ten nine other times.

He gained nationwide attention when appearing in the NASCAR Winter Heat series, and was scheduled to join the Craftsman Truck Series in 1997.

On The Day In Question:
On Sunday February 9th, 1997, Trickle had enjoyed dinner with his girlfriend at a local restaurant. On the drive home, a friend called Trickle's cell and invited him to play tennis. He arranged to meet his friend at a lighted court. It was then around 9:00pm.

On his way to the courts, Trickle stopped briefly at home (he lived with his parents) to change into athletic gear, and then left again. On his way to the tennis courts, a car pulled alongside his on a freeway and fired shots into his car.

Trickle was hit in the head, but did not die immediately. He would spend over a year in the hospital and die from complications of his wounds 409 days after the shooting. Just before he died, Trickle seemed to come out of his coma, talking to friends and relatives briefly before slumping back into unconsciousness.

Investigation:
From the beginning of the case, police were left with few leads. The shooting occurred on a darkened underpass. Although a potential witness came forward months after the shooting with a description of a car they had seen in the area, police have never named a suspect or arrested anyone in relation to the shooting.

Trickle had no enemies or anyone that would want to harm him, that friends and family could recall. In fact, just three months before his death he had been presented with an award naming him as the series' most popular driver. The award was peer voted.

At the time of Trickle's death, the law limited the prosecution of murder to a maximum of year and a day. Because Trickle's death occurred more than a year after the shooting, it could not be prosecuted as a murder.

Current Status:
Trickle's death prompted a change in the law surrounding the time limit for murder prosecutions. In 1999, the state of Nevada passed a law removing the time limit on prosecution of murder cases.

In 2001 Trickle became the biological father to twins Cole and Joelyn, born after his death with in vitro fertilization. His sperm was taken before his death with the idea that his girlfriend would one day carry his children.

In the end though, she could not go through with it, and a family friend asked if they could carry on Chris' lineage instead.

Other members of his family continue to be involved in racing. His family has offered a $35,000 reward to anyone who provides information leading to the killer.

His murder remains unsolved.

The Lane Bryant Murder Spree: A Robbery Gone Bad

Victims: Connie R. Woolfolk, Sarah T. Szafranski, Carrie Hudek Chiuso, Rhoda McFarland, Jennifer L. Bishop
Date: February 2nd, 2008
Location: Tinley Park, Illinois
Suspect: None

Backstory:
The Lane Bryant killings took place on February 8th, 2008, in the Lane Bryant store in a small clothing outlet in the suburb of Tinley Park, Illinois.

On The Day In Question:
That morning, four customers were visiting the store. A part time employee and the store manager were working. Shortly after 10:45am, police received an emergency call from the store's manager. A police officer had been only a few hundred yards away at the time of the call and was at the store moments afterwards. However, it was already too late.

At the store police discovered that only the part time employee had survived a brutal attack, but was herself badly injured. The four customers and the manager had all been shot dead.

The four customers were all in their twenties or thirties and the manager was forty-two years old.

Investigation:
The part time employee (her identity has been withheld by police) described the gunman as a tall black man with thick cornrow braided hair and a receding hairline. She mentioned that he had one braid lying over the side of his face, decorated with four light green beads.

He was at least six feet tall, and had broad shoulders with a husky build. He posed as a deliveryman when entering the store, before announcing his intent to rob the store. He then bound the six women in the back room.

Police locked down the shopping center temporarily, but it was reopened once it was established that the gunman had already left the scene.

Investigators have received over 7,000 tips since 2008, and spent $2 million on the investigation. There is a reward of $100,000 being offered for information leading to the arrest of the killer. Despite these efforts, no one has ever been charged with the crime.

Early in the investigation, detectives discovered a connection between the manager of the store and the leader of a church that she was involved in as the associate pastor. She and the pastor had been involved in an argument over a six-figure mortgage on the church, and he had started a new congregation in Texas. However, when investigated the lead did not generate any arrests.

Sightings of the offender, based on a sketch created from a description from the injured part time worker, have been reported from all over the country. However, none of the tips have ever amounted to anything.

Police believe that the killings were likely a robbery gone wrong with an inexperienced offender. The store would not have held a large amount of cash, and the killing of the store's customers was unusual.

Current Status:
For years, the former Lane Bryant store remained vacant in the shopping center. In November 2013, a TJ Maxx store moved into the property. Although they claim they were unaware of the property's history, the store made a donation in honor of the victims of the Lane Bryant killings.

In the next five years since the killings, Tinely Park had only two further homicides, and in both police made arrests within hours of the crimes. The case of the Lane Bryant killings remains the largest mass killing in the town, and also remains unsolved to this day.

The Jefferson Davis Eight: Victims of the Same Person?

Victims: Jeff Davis 8
Dates: 2005-2009
Location: Jefferson Davis Parish, Jennings, Louisiana
Suspects: Frankie Richard, Bryon Chad Jones, Lawrence Nixon, local law enforcement officers

Backstory:
The case of the Jeff Davis 8 is actually a series of murders between 2005 and 2009 in the Jefferson Davis Parish of Louisiana.

The victims were all women, and all involved in some way in prostitution and/or drugs. By the time the bodies were recovered, they were mostly decomposed to the point that the cause of death was unable to be determined.

The victims were Lynn Lewis, 28, Ernestine Marie Daniels Patterson, 30, Kristen Gary Lopez, 21, Whitnei Dubois, 26, Laconia Brown, 23, Crystal Shay Benoit Zeno, 24, Brittney Gary, 17, and Necole Guillory, 26.

On The Day In Question:
The first victim, Lewis, was found floating in the Grand Marais Canal by an angler on May 20th, 2005. Her body was decomposed, and showed no evidence of injury except for a small patch of blood under her scalp.

Between 2005 and 2009, the bodies of seven more women were found in the swamps and canals surrounding the town of Jennings, Louisiana. Given that the entire town's population was only around 10,000, seven murders were certainly staggering.

It was determined that the victims Patterson and Brown had their throats slit. Decomposition was too advanced in the other victims to accurately determine cause of death, but the suspected cause is asphyxia (suffocation).

Investigation:
It wasn't until December of 2008 that a taskforce was established to investigate the crimes. It consisted of fourteen federal, state, and local law enforcement agencies. From the beginning, they were focused on finding a serial killer for all the murders.

A reward of $35,000 was issued for information leading to the guilty party's arrest. It was later increased to $85,000.

Four people have either been arrested or had warrants issued for their arrest in relation to the murders. Two people were held for months on charges of murder, before being released due to evidence issues.

An investigation into the killings by author and investigative reporter Ethan Brown discovered multiple connections between the victims. Some were related (Lopez and Gary were cousins), while others lived together (Gary and Benoit).

The women had also all acted as police informants regarding the local drug trade. They also provided information about other victims of the Jeff Davis 8 before they too were killed.

Brown is also highly critical of the local police and the taskforce. He states that it should have been obvious that the murders were not committed by a serial killer. The women all knew each other well, and were involved heavily in the local prostitution and drug scene.

Brown states that serial killings generally involve victims with no visible relationship to the offender. Brown states that information he gained during his own investigation reveals connections between lead suspects across the multiple murders.

Frankie Richard, who was a strip club owner and also suspected of dealing drugs, admitted to being addicted to crack cocaine, and having sex at one time or another with most of the victims. He has been reported as one of the last people to see Lopez alive.

Bryon Chad Jones and Lawrence Nixon (Brown's cousin) were both briefly charged with second-degree murder in the case of Patterson's murder.

In both of these cases however, suggested misconduct and corruption in the sheriff's office lead to charges being dropped or dismissed. Richard has been linked to the sheriff's office by witnesses who are themselves involved in law enforcement. It has also been claimed by two inmates that the sheriff's office deliberately disposed of evidence at Richard's request.

In the case of Jones and Nixon, the sheriff's office did not perform any testing at the crime scene until fifteen months after the crime was committed. Not surprisingly, the tests failed to demonstrate the presence of blood. Could things have ever been more convoluted or mishandled?

No one has ever been convicted in any of the eight murder cases.

Current Status:
In 1990, two men stole over 300 pounds of marijuana from the sheriff's office. Brown's investigation revealed that court documents relating to the theft named Richard as an accomplice, along with a man named Ted Gary, who was then at the time the chief deputy sheriff. Neither man was ever charged.

Then, in 1993, Sheriff Dallas Cormier pled guilty to one count of obstruction of justice in federal court. He was charged with various crimes, including improper dealings with inmates, and using public funds to buy personal items including trucks, tires, and guns.

Other scandals have also hit the Jennings' Sheriff's Office. These include claims of illegal traffic stops, and a civil rights lawsuit brought against the police chief and other male police officers by eight female police officers. They claimed widespread acts of sexual harassment and violence, including forced oral sex.

Again, in 2013 a former Jennings police chief was charged after a police audit found $4,500 in cash, along with a large stash of drugs missing from the police evidence locker.

Claims that high-ranking officers in the Jennings police force covered up the murders, therefore, do not seem too far-fetched. A Sergeant named Jesse Ewing interviewed two female inmates over the claims in 2007.

Worried that his recording of the claims would just 'disappear', he handed the interview tapes over to a local private investigator, who then gave them to the FBI.

However, the tapes were simply returned to the local task force. Apparently unrelated, Ewing then found himself being charged with malfeasance in office and sexual misconduct against one of the women he interviewed. He denies any involvement and the charge of sexual misconduct was dismissed. After more than twenty years on the job, Ewing's position was terminated.

Brown claims to have listened to the tapes. He reports that they offer specific information regarding the murders of Dubois and Lopez. The tapes include details of a local law enforcement cover up of Richard's involvement in at least one of the murders. He has withheld any names or details to protect the witnesses.

The inmates also claimed that Richard transported the body of Lopez inside a barrel in a truck that was later purchased by Warren Gary, the sheriff's chief criminal investigator. It's alleged that Richard and Gary both washed the truck out afterwards. Public records corroborate the purchase of the truck.

Gary was fined $10,000 by the Louisiana Board of Ethics for purchasing the truck. Gary had purchased it from Connie Siler, a known associate of Richard. He then resold it for 50% profit less than one month later. Siler used the profits from the sale to pay for a bad check she had written.

She had been questioned by the sheriff's office in relation to the bad checks case.
Brown further calls the motives of law enforcement into question with the discovery that at least one of the victims of the Jeff Davis 8 witnessed the killing of a civilian by law enforcement during a drug bust.

In April of 2005 law enforcement officers (including probation officers and detectives), acting on a tip, raided a home in Jennings. A man named Leonard Crochet was found standing in the corner of the room. When Crochet made a sudden movement, a parole officer fired and killed him.

When the scene was investigated however, police were unable to find any evidence of a weapon on his person or in the immediate vicinity. Neither would anyone else present at the time testify that Crochet had a weapon when he was shot. The probation officer was charged with negligent homicide, but a grand jury failed to indict him.

Many people, including Richard himself, have commented that the victims of the Jeff Davis 8 had been present during the raid where Crochet was killed. Were the police trying to cover up the illegal killing of a suspect by one of their own?

Finally, a review of task force documents revealed that despite the same names (all local law enforcement) being mentioned multiple times in investigations, the allegations were never made public, nor were any of the named officers arrested or questioned.

The murders have not yet been investigated by a third party outside the taskforce.

Conclusion

One can't help but feel for the victims and their loved ones left behind. To not know the perpetrators of these terrible crimes and to never see them brought to justice must be some of the worst of tortures to be endured.

By continuing to put the spotlight on these crimes, the chances of solving some them increases and there is always hope.

Dear Readers,

Thank you for purchasing this book. I enjoyed researching and writing about these cases and I hope you found them to be both interesting and engrossing.

If your friends and family would enjoy reading about this topic, please be sure to let them know about this book.

Again, thank you for your support and I look forward to writing more books of Murders Unsolved.

Regards,
Mike Riley

Be sure to check out Mike's other books:

America's Early Serial Killers: Five Cases of Frontier Madness
"We tend to think of those early settlers as hard working, decent people only looking for religious freedom and better opportunities for their families. However, even during those times, people existed who were depraved, evil and mentally ill. These are some of their stories."
Check it out on Amazon in the Kindle eBooks Category

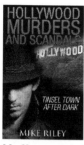

Hollywood Murders and Scandals: Tinsel Town After Dark

"In the late afternoon, her friends recalled, Monroe began to act strangely seeming to be heavily under the influence. She made statements to friend Peter Lawford that he should tell the President goodbye and tell himself goodbye."

Check it out on Amazon in the Kindle eBooks Category

Made in the USA
Middletown, DE
28 September 2018